Red, White, and Black

Symposium on Indians in the Old South

CHARLES M. HUDSON, Editor

Southern Anthropological Society Proceedings, No. 5

SOUTHERN ANTHROPOLOGICAL SOCIETY
Distributed by the University of Georgia Press
Athens 30601

SOUTHERN ANTHROPOLOGICAL SOCIETY

Founded 1966

Officers 1970-71

Copyright © 1971 by
Southern Anthropological Society
LC 70-156041
SBN 8203-0308-9
Printed in the United States

Contents

Preface

THIS symposium was presented at the 1970 meeting of the Southern Anthropological Society in Athens, Georgia. Its purpose was to explore a subject on which anthropologists have been strangely silent: the Indians of the Old South. Although the Indians of the southeastern United States probably achieved the most complex social and cultural development north of Mexico, and although the Old South was a fascinating and richly documented complex society, our knowledge of both still contains large gaps. Indeed, in organizing this symposium I often encountered extreme difficulty in finding scholars who were willing or able to write papers on some of the subjects that had to be covered. So far as I could determine, disregarding conferences and symposia on Southeastern prehistory, no attempt has ever been made to bring anthropologists and other scholars together on the subject of Indians in the Old South. Therefore, it seemed particularly appropriate that the key symposium of the 1970 meeting of the Southern Anthropological Society be devoted to surveying what we know about the Southern Indians and to charting directions for future research. The symposium was organized with the assumption that the Old South was a complex society and consequently that successful research on it must be thoroughly multidisciplinary, requiring the skills and interests of anthropologists, sociologists, historians, geographers, linguists, and others.

All of the papers in this volume were presented at the symposium itself except the paper by John H. Peterson, Jr., written especially for this volume, and the paper by William S. Willis, Jr., reprinted from *The Journal of Negro History*. One hopes that these essays will make it clear that the Old South is an area where interesting and relevant anthropological research can be conducted. It can even be argued that the South is an area where anthropologists might gain insight into the ethical and moral assumptions that are now troubling their field. For example, the reluctance of social anthropologists to teach and do research in the South is puzzling in view of their ready willingness to do research in politically repressive societies in all parts of the world.

Many individuals helped in the planning and organization of this symposium. Charles Wynes gave me advice and encouragement from the very outset, and I regret that I was not able to succeed in following through on more of his suggestions. I am grateful to Marion Rice and Wilfrid Bailey and the Anthropology Curriculum Project for financial assistance. The following individuals generously gave me advice on particular matters: Clarence Bacote, Brewton Berry, W. Roger Buffalohead, Rupert Costo, Edward Dozier, Clement Eaton, Edward T. Price, Edgar Thompson, and the late James Mc-Bride Dabbs. And for various contributions to the symposium and its outcome I am grateful to Andrew Dreadfulwater, Peter B. Hammond, Scott McLemore, Hubert Ross, Robert Thomas, and Susan Tate. The symposium would have been far less successful had it not been for the hard work of David Hally, program chairman; Walter Ward, local arrangements chairman; and George S. Brooks and the staff of the Georgia Center for Continuing Education. As usual, I am grateful to my wife, Joyce Rockwood Hudson, and her Pollyanna-Episcopal world view.

Charles Hudson
SAS Editor

Introduction

CHARLES HUDSON

THREE Indians were once out hunting. One went after water and found a nice hole of water but was afraid to drink. Another went down to it, dipped his fingers in, and said, "It is good. Let us go into it." So he dived in and came out. When he came out he was white. From him came the white people. The second dived in and came out darker because the water was somewhat [muddy]. From him came the Indians. The third dived in and came out black because the water was now very [muddy]. From him came the Negroes. Just before the first man dived he felt of the rocks and they rattled. He did not tell the others that this was gold. They went on from there and the Indian found something else. The white man was told about this and he picked it up. It was a book. He asked the Indian to read this but he could not. The white man, however, could read it, and it was to tell him about this gold. The book gave him this advantage. "The Nokfilas (whites) were terrible people to take the lead."[1]

In preliterate societies people carry all they know about the past in their heads.[2] This means that they must forget a great deal, committing to tradition only the events that are socially most relevant. Anthropologists who have done research on the historical traditions of preliterate people have found that they do not exclude facts from history randomly, but rather by a process that has been called "structural amnesia" (Barnes 1947; Goody 1968). This means that those events which have little relevance to the structure of their society are relegated to historical oblivion. For example, in preliterate societies in which one's social position depends upon one's genealogy, it is obviously impossible to remember all of one's ancestors. What usually happens is that people in such societies have clear traditions about their most remote ancestors, who lived in mythical time before the present world order began, and they have similarly clear traditions about their ancestors in recent generations, but the genealogy in be-

1

tween is "telescoped." The ancestors in between are shifted around and dropped from memory, the victims of social irrelevance or changed conditions. Traditions about the remote, original ancestors are ideological charters for relationships with various outgroups (strangers, foreigners, enemies), while traditions about the recently dead govern most day-to-day, in-group relationships (kinsmen, neighbors). The ancestors in between, neither distant nor close, bear upon relationships which are ambivalent or changing.

A somewhat different kind of structural amnesia can be seen in the history of the Old South. The whites in the South have had a well-known monopoly on power and wealth, and the history they have written is so white it has become embarrassing. When blacks or Indians show up in the history of the Old South, they show up as objects or as background features, and more often than not they do not show up at all. On the other hand, when one reads the accounts that anthropologists and Indian historians have written about the same period, they are pure red; the whites mostly show up as outsiders, invading and destroying, and the blacks are even less evident here than in the work by white historians. Moreover, the recent florescence of research by black historians, realigning and amplifying history to fit the changing social order in the modern South, is too black, this being an understandable bias, but a bias nonetheless.

What this Southern structural amnesia misses, of course, is that the Old South was a complex social entity composed of three races—red, white, and black, leaving aside for the moment various mixtures—and these racial divisions were cross-cut with cultural and economic divisions. Any approach to Southern history which fails to take account of these complexities in the larger social situation must necessarily fail to adequately account for any major part of the history of the Old South. Although we are like our preliterate brothers in having a biased view of the past, our being literate makes us different from them in enabling us to recover something of the past and examine it anew. And in view of recent social changes in the South and in the rest of the country, this is an opportune time to do some historical re-thinking.

Toward achieving a more comprehensive anthropological and historical understanding of the Old South, the first part of this volume consists of papers surveying research in several specialized approaches to the past, namely two specialized fields of anthropology—physical anthropology and archaeology—and two fields closely related to anthropology—geography and linguistics. Although some historians may question the relevance of these approaches, many other historians are increasingly realizing along with anthropologists that we need to explore every avenue to the past that is available to us. As Louis De Vorsey shows in his paper in this volume, the Old South is a historical period upon which the historical geographer and the anthropologist can fruitfully collaborate, each amplifying the results of the other. Anthropologists have always been concerned with the relationship between man and the natural world, but they have not kept up with historical geographers in exploring all of the different sources which hold this information, and especially they have neglected old maps. De Vorsey calls for collaboration between geography and anthropology like that advocated by Carl O. Sauer and Alfred L. Kroeber at Berkeley several decades ago.

Like De Vorsey, William Pollitzer is concerned with reconstructing a feature of the natural world in the Old South, namely the biological characteristics of the Southern Indians, their morphology, classification, and evolution. Again echoing De Vorsey, he calls for a kind of collaboration between physical anthropologists and scholars in other fields that is all too rare. The complexity of the Old South is evident in Pollitzer's review of research on the physical anthropology of the Southern Indians. Not only were there significant biological differences among the Southern Indians, but the human genetics of the Old South was also complicated by the interbreeding of Indians with whites and blacks.

In Mary Haas's succinct survey of research on Southeastern Indian languages we see that the Old South was also diverse with respect to the languages that were spoken. In fact, she underscores the little known fact that in all of North America the Southeast was second in linguistic diversity only to the west coast of the United States and Canada. The languages spoken by the Southern Indians belonged to no less than four language families, containing languages as different from each other as English is different from Mandarin Chinese, and moreover we have some evidence on about a half dozen additional languages, most of which are remotely related to these four families, but some are perhaps related to even further language families. And the linguistic diversity in the Old South does not end here. Considerable dialectical variation, both social and regional, existed in the English spoken by the colonists (Brooks 1935; Kurath and McDavid 1961; Stephenson 1968), not to speak of French, Spanish, and German, the former remaining an important language in Louisiana to this day (Morgan 1960; McDavid 1967). The black slaves brought here from Africa spoke a variety of African languages (Turner 1949); and an argot derived from Irish Gaelic (Harper and Hudson n.d.) was introduced into the South in the nineteenth century. With all this in mind it would be foolish to conclude that linguistic diversity in the Old South ends here.

That difficult area where prehistoric archaeology touches history is surveyed in this volume by David Hally. Here, even more than elsewhere, collaboration between anthropologists and historians is essential. Good archaeology is both expensive and time-consuming, and Hally makes it clear that both money and time for extensive archaeological excavation of historically identified sites are desperately needed. And this need is made all the more acute as sites are progressively destroyed by pot hunters, construction companies, and the Corps of Engineers. We could almost regard the scandalous destruction of archaeological sites in the South as a second Indian removal. In the first removal we got rid of the Indians, and in the second removal we are wiping out their last *in situ* traces, aborting their last feeble chances of winning a place in history.

Archaeology has had a rather secure place in the Southeast for some time, but an indigenous ethnology or social anthropology (the terms can be used interchangeably) is quite recent. Archaeology took root early for several reasons. For one thing, the large mounds and the "moundbuilder" myths that grew up around them in the Southeast were invitations to treasure-hunters and collectors, thus making a lasting impression on the general public. Along with this the idea of excavating antiquities appealed to elitist intellectuals. Moreover, poverty in the South was an indirect stimulus to archaeology: the first large scale excavations were supported by the TVA and the WPA during the Depression as an ideal way to spend money on "nonproductive" labor. Looking at the other side of the coin, one factor that slowed the development of social anthropology was that it directly challenged the racist ideology that troubled the South in the past and continues to do so in lesser degree in the present (Willis 1970:37). Thus, the social anthropology that has been done on the aboriginal peoples of the South has been rather like that in an underdeveloped country today, namely the social anthropologists doing the research were all outsiders who carefully avoided asking too many embarrassing questions. The most important social anthropological research on the Southern Indians has been done by three men: Frank Speck, a professor of anthropology at the University of Pennsylvania whose main work was with the Catawbas (e.g., 1913; 1934; 1935; 1939) and the Yuchis (1909); James Mooney, from the Smithsonian, who did excellent ethnographic and historical research on the

Cherokees (e.g., 1891; 1900); and John Swanton, also from the Smithsonian, whose favorite people were the Creeks (e.g., 1922; 1928a; 1928b), but who did research on many other groups in the Southeast (e.g., 1911; 1928c), and who wrote several basic works dealing with the Southeast as a whole (e.g., 1929; 1946).[3]

Our debt to these three social anthropologists can scarcely be exaggerated, but their work suffers from some startling blind spots. One shortcoming is that they examined Indian societies as if they were isolated social entities, existing apart from a complex Southern society. The fact is, the Southern Indians began losing their autonomy as soon as they became entangled in the fur trade, enslaved by planters, or involved as combatants in colonial rivalries. Moreover, as William Willis has pointed out, with few exceptions social anthropologists literally turned their heads the other way to avoid blacks in the South (1970:34).

This is the reason why the second part of this symposium takes the form it does. Our understanding of the Southern Indians and of other social and cultural groups in the Old South will be deficient until we come to understand the complex social situation in which they were all participants. As soon as we begin apprehending it as a complex system, we begin to appreciate some of the striking gaps in Southern history which exist in spite of the great amount that has been written on the subject. One searches Southern history in vain for an adequate account of the mixed-bloods whose descendants live in fairly sizable numbers in the South today;[4] one finds surprisingly little coverage of the Indians themselves, particularly those who remained in the South after removal; and the historians tell us rather less than we would like to know about the non-Plantation whites (Owsley 1949).

The basic structure of society in the Old South resembled the structure of the so-called "plural societies," for the most part products of European colonialism, which economists and anthropologists have decribed in various parts of the world and which may date back to the period of Roman expansion or even earlier (Smith 1965; Morris 1967; Despres 1968). Namely, the Old South consisted of people categorized into several distinct social and cultural sections, each with distinctive social institutions, broadly divisible into red, white, and black, who lived in the same place but who did not mix (at least, not in socially approved ways), and one of these sections, the whites, held a monopoly on power which became more absolute as time went on. One would not wish to draw this parallel between the Old South and various European colonial societies too far, but certainly the comparison gives us categories of social understanding we would not otherwise have (Hudson 1970:52-80). Calling the Old South plural carries with it the recognition that it conformed to this ideal type more closely in the middle period of its history than in the early colonial period or in more recent times, and calling the Old South a society carries with it the recognition that it was beset with deep divisions and bitter conflict.

The apex of society in the Old South was occupied by whites, and the apex of white society was occupied by planters who owned large amounts of land and many black slaves. As F. N. Boney argues in his paper in this volume, when the Southern mystique is stripped away these men were basically capitalists who were out to make a buck. Though small in number, their right to control things, while not absolute, was rarely questioned. The political ascendancy of the planters depended upon their being able to perpetuate the divisions within society while not allowing them to break out in uncontrollable conflict. For example, the planters recognized a possible revolutionary threat in the whites who were less well off than they. This was not so much the case with yeoman farmers operating family farms in the back country, who were occasionally opposed to black slavery but even more opposed to free blacks. But as Joseph Brent points out, the freedmen (poor whites who had worked out their period of indenture) and their descendants were a different matter. Because there was no place for them in the structure of the plantation economy, their alienation was always a threat. Many·of them had come from the slums and prisons of England, and they carried with them attitudes and beliefs learned there. So long as social mobility was possible, they imitated their former masters and tried to become rich and powerful themselves. The poor whites were further appeased by the presence of a large and utterly powerless class of black slaves to which all whites, however poor, felt superior and, hence, in some sense equal to other whites.

The relations between whites and Indians varied as time went on. In general, the whites only tolerated the Indians so long as they had a use for them. They exploited the Indians first of all in the fur trade, and also as slaves, but as slaves they were never as satisfactory as blacks were, partly because when they escaped they could easily live off the land and find refuge with their fellows (Lauber 1913). The more powerful tribes or "nations," as they were called, were useful allies in the rivalry among the English, French, and Spanish colonists. However, John Peterson makes the point that as soon as this rivalry drew to a close, the Indians' days were numbered. It then became expedient to "remove" them to the West, expropriate their land, and turn it over to whites. As Joseph Brent points out, this was yet another way the white elite had of buying off dissatisfaction among the non-plantation whites. Not all of the Indians went west, though the ones who remained behind could live only a precarious existence as squatters on marginal land. Peterson discusses the fact that very little is known about this phase of the history of the Southern Indians, and he is perhaps the first to clearly perceive the dilemma of these Indians who remained behind. It was simply that they could neither be white land-owners nor black slaves, and this left them with essentially nothing.

The relationship between white masters and black slaves has been examined in great detail by historians. What is perhaps not so well known is the fact that even in the early eighteenth century South Carolinians were as afraid of slave revolts as they were of hostile Indians. And the slaves did revolt, the Nat Turner rebellion being only the most well known of several. As a defensive measure, the whites took elaborate precautions to keep the blacks ignorant and divided, even to the point of denying them membership in Christianity.

What the whites feared most was an alliance between blacks and Indians. William Willis in an article reprinted in this volume presents evidence that the whites carried out a policy of divide and conquer by setting the Indians against the blacks, just as they had a more explicit policy of setting Indians against Indians. Nor was this policy of creating antagonisms between blacks and Indians limited to the English: in 1730 Governor Perrier of New France ordered black slaves to attack and kill the handful of surviving Chawasha Indians for the ulterior purpose of creating hostility between the races (Swanton 1911:30-31). Proof that the fear of red-black alliances was well founded came in the bloody Second Seminole War, lasting from 1835 until 1842, in which escaped black slaves and Seminole Indians fought the whites to a standstill in a long, tenacious war somewhat reminiscent of the American military involvement in Viet Nam. When some Southern Indians, notably the Cherokees, themselves adopted the institution of black slavery along with other aspects of Southern culture, the whites must have had mixed feelings. It must have pleased them because the Indians set themselves against the blacks by enslaving them, but it must have angered them because the Indians were by the same token becoming uppity (Abel 1915-1925).

Understanding the Old South as a social system is only part of the problem. The other task is to understand the ideological superstructure of this social system (Jordan 1968). Indeed it can be

argued that the ideology of the Old South was more "peculiar" than
the institution of slavery itself. Joseph Brent comments on the dual-
ism in white thought, the opposition of white to black, and the opposition of both of these to red, a category of humanity that was
literally thought to be a part of nature. In Southern thought these
were "pure" categories, each associated with a distinct stereotype.
It is for this reason, perhaps, that the mixed-bloods—people like the
Lumbee of North Carolina, the Brass Ankles of South Carolina, the
Melungeons of Tennessee, the Cajans of Alabama, the Redbones of
Louisiana, and many others—have always been such puzzling, "mys-
terious" people (Price 1953; Berry 1963). Because they were anomalous
with respect to fundamental categories, in some sense they threatened
to introduce disorder and chaos into the social universe. They were
not white, but they refused to be treated as blacks, and sometimes,
but not always, they refused to be treated as Indians, while at other
times they asked to be treated as Indians but were refused. Their
solution usually was to stay off to themselves, living poor lives on
marginal land, much as the Indians who escaped removal did. They
are still very much present in the contemporary South, and in many
cases their social isolation continues, as illustrated by the fact that
the names by which they are known generally have local significance
only. It should be obvious that "mixed-blood," as used here, designates
a social category rather than mere genetic intermixture. This becomes
clear when we realize that a number of individuals whose parents
were of different races (usually a white father and an Indian mother)
became prominent among the Southeastern Indians. Some of them became wealthy planters, owning large planations and many slaves.

    In general the white stereotype of the Indian was more variable
than that of the black. F. N. Boney mentions the fact that Thomas
Jefferson admired certain features of the Indians' stereotype and suggested that it would be a good thing if poor whites would take Indian
wives. Even elite whites could admit to having a trace of Indian blood,
though it was better if it came from a "noble" strain. Perhaps Jefferson could hold this rather charitable view because Virginia had
long since solved her "Indian problem." Other elite whites who were
closer to the frontier regarded Indians as little better than animals.

    Perhaps the most fruitful way of counteracting the Southern
structural amnesia discussed earlier is to scrutinize the official ideology
of the Old South and the elaborate fictions which preserved its in-
tegrity, and to use this as a basis for calling existing historical
knowledge and interpretation into question. One ideological assumption in the Old South was that the Indians were a part of nature, and

like beasts they were naturally blood-thirsty, killing for the pleasure of it. Are we to accept this as an explanation of why the Southern Indians were so divided among themselves? What was behind the political divisions among the Southern Indians? Are we to accept A. L. Kroeber's explanation of low aboriginal population in the Southeast as being a result of insane, constantly attritional warfare (Kroeber 1939)?

Another ideological assumption was that the Indians naturally hated the blacks, and the blacks, poor superstitious things, were naturally terrified of Indians. Some evidence suggests that this line of thought explains why South Carolinians tolerated Indians within their borders long after they had the means to drive them out. The rationale was that the Indians could be used as instruments to intimidate the blacks (Hudson 1970:56-58; Willis 1970:45). But was the handful of impoverished Catawbas in early nineteenth century South Carolina as fierce and as loathing of blacks as they were believed to be? And were the blacks truly terrified when an Indian approached? Was the Second Seminole War (sometimes called the Negro and Indian war) as inconsequential as most Southern histories would lead us to believe? Why were the Creeks and Seminoles more tolerant of escaped blacks than the Cherokees were (Willis 1970)?

A further assumption was that the Indians should be kept apart from the poor whites because the Indians, as innocent children of nature, would be corrupted by the uncouth ways of the whites. Historians have, of course, already asked whether elite whites did the Southern Indians a favor by "removing" them to safety on the other side of the Mississippi River, far from the unseemly ways of white trash. We may also ask whether these poor whites did not acquire much valuable knowledge from the Indians, and whether this knowledge did not in fact make a significant contribution to Southern culture. A considerable number of people with a European cultural background, black, white, and mixed-bloods, moved in and lived among the Indians even though doing so was illegal or disapproved. What kinds of social relationships existed between these people and their Indian hosts?

It would be unwise to claim that what has been suggested here is a cure-all for Southern structural amnesia. Perhaps the most important message of the papers included in this volume is that the Old South was full of cultural and social complexities, and that although these complexities are usually concealed or forgotten, many of them can be inquired into and explained in a systematic fashion. And just as one can learn a great deal about the structure of a tent by studying the wrinkles in its fabric, one can learn much about the structure of the Old South by studying these complexities. In particular, further research on the mixed-bloods promises to tell us much about the nature of the Old South. A second message is that if there was ever a fit subject for multidisciplinary research, it is the Old South. Much research remains to be done, and it should be done from as many intellectual vantage points as possible.

NOTES

1. A Creek Indian myth collected by John Swanton (1929:75). It is probably incomplete.
2. I am grateful to Wilfrid Bailey, F. N. Boney, David Hally, and Michael Olien, who read and criticized this introductory essay. However, I alone am responsible for its content.
3. Additional and generally more recent contributions to the ethnography and history of the Southern Indians have come from Leonard Broom, Fred Eggan, Charles Fairbanks, Raymond Fogelson, William Gilbert, John Goggin, John Gulick, Harriet Kupferer, Alexander Spoehr, William Sturtevant, and others. About one-third of them can claim to be "indigenous" social anthropologists, this being some measure of the development of the underdeveloped South.
4. But see the recent study of the Coe Ridge people of Kentucky by William Lynwood Montell (1970) and forthcoming research by Peter B. Hammond.

REFERENCES

Abel, Annie Heloise, 1915-1925. *Slaveholding Indians,* 3 vols. (Cleveland: Arthur C. Clark Company).
Barnes, J. A., 1947. The Collection of Genealogies. *Rhodes-Livingstone Journal: Human Problems in British Central Africa,* V.
Berry, Brewton, 1963. *Almost White* (New York: Macmillan).
Brooks, Cleanth, 1935. *The Relation of the Alabama-Georgia Dialect to the Provincial Dialects of Great Britain* (Baton Rouge: Louisiana State University Press).
Despres, Leo A., 1968. Anthropological Theory, Cultural Pluralism, and the Study of Complex Societies. *Current Anthropology* 9:3-16.
Goody, Jack (ed.), 1968. *Literacy in Traditional Societies* (Cambridge: At the University Press).
Harper, Jared and Charles Hudson, n.d. Irish Traveler Cant. *Journal of English Linguistics,* in press.
Hudson, Charles, 1970. *The Catawba Nation* (Athens, Georgia: University of Georgia Press).
Jordan, Winthrop D., 1968. *White Over Black: American Attitudes Toward the Negro, 1550-1812* (Chapel Hill, N. C.: University of North Carolina Press).
Kroeber, Alfred L., 1939. *Cultural and Natural Areas of Native North America,* University of California Publications in American Archaeology and Ethnology, Vol. 38 (Berkeley: University of California Press).
Kurath, Hans and Raven I. McDavid, 1961. *The Pronunciation of English in the Atlantic States* (Ann Arbor: University of Michigan Press, 1961).
Lauber, Almon Wheeler, 1913. *Indian Slavery in Colonial Times Within the Present Limits of The United States* (New York: Columbia University Press).
McDavid, Raven I., 1967. Needed Research in Southern Dialects. In *Perspectives*

on the South: Agenda for Research, Edgar T. Thompson ed. (Durham, N. C.: Duke University Press), pp. 113-124.

Montell, William Lynwood, 1970. *The Saga of Coe Ridge: A Study in Oral History* (Knoxville: University of Tennessee Press).

Morgan, Raleigh, 1960. The Lexicon of St. Martin Creole. *Anthropological Linguistics* 2:7-29.

Mooney, James, 1891. *The Sacred Formulas of the Cherokees*. 7th Annual Report of the Bureau of American Ethnology (Washington: GPO), pp. 301-397.

———————, 1900. *Myths of the Cherokees*. 19th Annual Report of the Bureau of American Ethnology, Part 1 (Washington: GPO).

Morris, H. S., 1967. Some Aspects of the Concept Plural Society. *Man.* 2:169-184.

Owsley, Frank L., 1949. *Plain Folk of the Old South* (Baton Rouge: Louisiana State University Press, 1949).

Price, Edward T., 1953. A Geographic Analysis of White-Negro-Indian Racial Mixtures in Eastern United States. *Annals of the Association of American Geographers* 43:138-155.

Smith, M. G., 1965. *The Plural Society in the British West Indies* (Berkeley, Los Angeles: University of California Press).

Speck, Frank, 1909. *Ethnology of the Yuchi Indians*. Anthropological Publications of the University Museum, University of Pennsylvania, Vol. 1, No. 1 (Philadelphia).

———————, 1913. Some Catawba Texts and Folklore. *The Journal of American Folklore* 26:319-330.

———————, 1934. *Catawba Texts*. Columbia University Contributions to Anthropology, Vol. 24 (New York: Columbia University Press).

———————, 1935. Siouan Tribes of the Carolinas as Known from Catawba, Tutelo, and Documentary Sources. *American Anthropologist* 37:201-225.

———————, 1939. The Catawba Nation and its Neighbors. *North Carolina Historical Review* 16:404-417.

Stephenson, Edward A., 1968. The Beginnings of the Loss of Postvocalic /r/ in North Carolina. *Journal of English Linguistics* 2:57-77.

Swanton, John, 1911. *Indian Tribes of the Lower Mississippi Valley and Adjacent Coast of the Gulf of Mexico*, Bureau of American Ethnology Bulletin No. 43 (Washington: GPO).

———————, 1922. *Early History of the Creek Indians and Their Neighbors*, Bureau of American Ethnology Bulletin No. 73 (Washington: GPO).

———————, 1928a. *Social Organization and Social Usages of the Indians of the Creek Confederacy*, 42nd Annual Report of the Bureau of American Ethnology (Washington GPO), pp. 23-472.

———————, 1928b. *Religious Beliefs and Medical Practices of the Creek Indians*, 42nd Annual Report of the Bureau of American Ethnology (Washington: GPO), pp. 473-672.

———————, 1928c. *Social and Religious Beliefs and Usages of the Chickasaw Indians*, 44th Annual Report of the Bureau of American Ethnology (Washington: GPO), pp. 169-273.

———————, 1929. *Myths and Tales of the Southeastern Indians*, Bureau of American Ethnology Bulletin No. 88 (Washington: GPO).

———————, 1946. *The Indians of the Southeastern United States*, Bureau of American Ethnology No. 137 (Washington: GPO).

Turner, Lorenzo D. *Africanisms in the Gullah Dialect* (Chicago: University of Chicago Press).

Willis, William S., Jr. 1970. Anthropology and Negroes on The Southern Colonial Frontier. In *The Black Experience in America*, James C. Curtis and Lewis L. Gould, eds. (Austin and London: University of Texas Press), pp. 33-50.

Part I

Early Maps As a Source in the Reconstruction of Southern Indian Landscapes

Louis De Vorsey, Jr.

In his recent review article entitled, "Geographic Perspectives In Anthropology," Marvin Mikesell, a geographer, convincingly demonstrated the many close links which have existed between the two man-oriented disciplines—geography and anthropology (1967). He stressed the youthfulness, common ancestry, and the common intellectual roots which have shaped their developments through the past three quarters of a century. Both anthropology and geography were shown to have served as valuable academic bridges in recurring attempts to span the widening gulf between the physical and social sciences.

The concept of culture, which has formed the keystone of anthropology's impressive structure, is increasingly recognized as occupying a like position in modern geography. The academic geographer of the present day has moved far from the overriding preoccupation with the determinative role of the physical environment which characterized his discipline four or five decades ago. Rather, he now tends to shape his research and quest for understanding into the form of questions which ask how a particular group perceives, organizes, and utilizes its physical environment or habitat at any given point in time. Man, operating within the context of a culture group, has emerged as the active agent in the modern geographer's study of areal differentiation. Most modern geographers would agree with Charles Frake in concluding that man is "unique among organisms, [carving] . . . his ecological niches primarily with cultural tools of his own invention rather than with biological specializations" (1962:53). In a large measure this new direction in geographical thought has been due to

12

the lessons which geographers have learned from anthropologists and others. Fortunately, American academic geography, like anthropology, has been characterized by a high degree of electicism.

Mikesell concluded his review by expressing concern over the paucity of examples of cooperative studies undertaken by workers in anthropology and geography. He mentioned the fact that over four decades have passed since the eminent geographer Carl O. Sauer called attention to the overlapping interests of geographers and anthropologists. Sauer, in 1925, suggested that a gradual coalescence of the disciplines might "represent the first of a series of fusions into a larger science of man" (Sauer 1963:350n). Mikesell found the absence of this fusion "regrettable but understandable." He observed that "even the most uninhibited scholar is constrained, to some extent, by professional affiliations and the departmental structure of our universities." The boundary separating anthropology and geography departments might be likened to many of those marking the map of modern Africa —more arbitrary than logical. This long-standing academic demarcation has encouraged introspective methodologies and what Mikesell referred to as the "academic counterpart to nationalism."

Academic "nationalism" has given way to "internationalism" in this symposium on Indians in the Old South. Anthropologists are here joined with historians, linguists, and geographers to gain insight into the life and rich culture of the South's first Americans.

HISTORICAL GEOGRAPHY AND HISTORICAL CARTOGRAPHY

Historical geography is a subfield of geography which has traditionally had strong ties with both anthropology and history. Currently the parameters and objectives of research in historical geography are the subject of lively debate by practitioners (Newcomb 1969). Most researchers cultivating this row of the geographic garden would, however, agree that the reconstruction of past landscapes is both a valid and important goal for their research (Broek 1932:7-10). It might be further asserted that the reconstruction of a region's landscape on the eve of its occupation by a new and distinctive culture group would be of considerable value to workers in a variety of disciplines including anthropology and history as well as geography. Such a reconstructed landscape could, in some measure, be viewed as the product of the culture group being dispossessed, in this case the Southern Indians during the eighteenth century. Similarly, such a reconstructed landscape might be employed as a datum base from which to gauge the impact of the dispossessing culture group in its regional setting through time. In our case the dispossessing group would be the Anglo-European cultivators and their African slaves of the same century.

In his attempt to reconstruct a landscape of the past, the historical geographer should employ as many relevant and illuminating sources as possible. The range of these sources is broad and their character is varied. Early maps, showing as they do the spatial arrangement of landscape features, are, however, of particular value as sources in any attempted reconstruction.

Early maps, like maps of the present day, are, in their primary conception, conventionalized pictures of the earth's surface as seen from above, to which lettering, symbols, and color are added for feature identification and clarity. The word "picture" is used here in its broadest sense to include what is believed about any area of earth space as well as what is cognized and objectively determined to exist in the area. Early maps, however, differ from modern maps in many important respects. In the words of R. A. Skelton they are, "the end-product of a complex series of processes—assembly of information from various sources and in different forms, both graphic and textual; assimilation to the mapmaker's geographical ideas, to transmitted cartographic patterns, or to his political interest; and the resultant stages of compilation, control, adjustment, and copying" (1965:4). The collection, study, and analysis of early maps are the essential elements of historical cartography. Historical cartography in turn is frequently an ancillary to the study of historical geography (Koeman 1968).

Researchers interested in past Southern Indian landscapes are fortunate in having an excellent guide to the early maps of the region. This is the volume entitled *The Southeast In Early Maps* (Cumming 1962). Also of considerable value as an introduction to the cartographic history of the South is Volume VI (1966) of the journal, *The Southeastern Geographer*. This was a special topic issue which contained articles by Cumming (1966), De Vorsey (1966a), Friis (1966), and Ristow (1966).

Early maps should be considered as extremely valuable historical documents which require somewhat specialized treatment in their reading and analysis (Harley 1968). As Skelton indicated in the statement quoted above, early maps were seldom if ever constructed out of the rigorously controlled processes of measurement and computation which are taken for granted in our scientifically compiled modern maps. As a result, they frequently show a mixture of fact and fiction, both of which can contribute to a clearer understanding of the geography of the past. Facts, such as coastlines, stream courses, animal licks, vegetation cover, roads, and settlements, are liable to change and alteration through time so a contemporary view of them at selected times in the past is indispensable (Coppock 1968).

Misconceptions such as the locating of deserts, lakes, rivers, and oceans where they did not exist in nature provide equally valuable insights. In this case, however, the insights afford a better appreciation of the motives, beliefs, and biases of those long departed individuals who lent life and significance to the landscapes of the past. Varrazano, in his passion to find an easy route to the Orient, reported the Carolina Outer Banks as a long narrow isthmus which blocked his entry to the "original sea . . . which is the one without doubt which goes about the extremity of India, China, and Cathay." Thus, in his mind the broad waters of Pamlico, Albermarle, and Core Sounds became the eastern margin of a beckoning ocean lapping the Oriental littoral somewhere to the west. This geographical misconception was an exciting idea to the sixteenth century European geographers and cartographers who heard it. It became incorporated in many maps of the period and did much to stimulate an interest in exploratory voyages and enterprises which led ultimately to the establishment of the Roanoke Colony (Cumming 1966:8). The satirist Swift drew attention to such cartographical shortcomings when he penned his now well known quatrain which read:

> So Geographers, in Afric Maps,
> With savage pictures fill their gaps,
> And, o'er inhabitable downs,
> Place elephants for want of towns.

Early maps can be viewed as "Cartographic Portraits" of regions of earth space. Just as a good portrait in its subjective rendering may reveal as much about the artist as about his subject, so an early map can reveal both the qualities of the landscape depicted and its author's background, training, and interests, in nearly equal measure. The understanding of early maps can be enhanced through a thorough knowledge of the historical circumstances surrounding their compilation and execution just as a viewer's appreciation of a portrait is enhanced by a knowledge of the painter and his school. The user of an early map, then, should not rest content with a superficial study of its content of lines and patterns. He should probe into the historical circumstances which surrounded its original creation by asking: Who was the cartographer? Why did he draw this particular map? For whom was this map originally intended? Answers to these and similar questions will enable the researcher to utilize these early "map documents" more effectively.

Early maps represent sources of inestimable value to the researcher interested in both the current and past cultural and physical landscapes of a region. They can show zones of change and dynamism as well as continuity and stability in those landscapes. They can show which features and patterns of the present scene are relics of past periods and conditions. They may suggest the reasons for present day patterns and relationships which are inexplicable in purely contemporary terms. They can help explain human actions and habits which are also not comprehensible in the light of present conditions alone. They can illustrate the process of human modification of the environment in a region. They can illustrate too, the process of natural change in a region. They can remind us of forgotten resources. Finally, they may help us all to come a bit closer to the civilizing realization that the present is but the past flowing into the future.

Employing Early Maps: Two Examples

Early maps exist in a wide variety of formats and scales, depending on the skill and intent of those original cartographers who created them. Some are little more than crude sketches while others are intricately detailed, amazingly accurate, and artistically executed. Some show broad regions or a whole continent while others depict small areas of only a few hundred acres or less. Rather than discuss maps in general terms only, it seems advisable to demonstrate their use and value in two recent attempts to reconstruct aspects of the mid-eighteenth century Southern Indian landscape. The first of these utilized a large number of small and medium scale manuscript and printed maps to reconstruct the boundary line which separated the British colonies from the Indian tribal lands in the pre-Revolutionary Southeast (De Vorsey 1966b). The second utilized many very large scale original surveyor's maps of granted properties, known as plats. With these large scale depictions of a relatively small study area, an attempt was made to reconstruct the aboriginal forest cover on the eve of occupation by eighteenth century European cultivators.

The Southern Indian Boundary Line—A Small Scale Study

At the outset of the American Revolution the Southern Indian Boundary Line separated the British colonies from the territory of the Indian tribes in the Southeast. The climactic twelve year period, which began with the surrender of almost all of the eastern portion of the

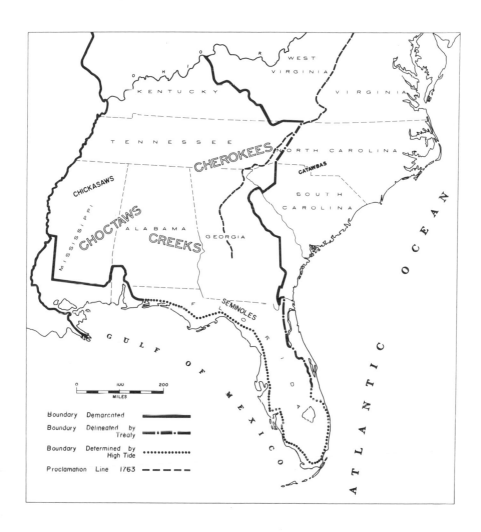

Figure 1. The Southern Indian Boundary Line on the Eve of the American Revolution. (Simplified from map on p. 232, *The Indian Boundary in the Southern Colonies, 1763-1775,* by Louis De Vorsey, Jr.).

continent by the French and Spanish in 1763, and ended with the political break between the seaboard colonies and the British Crown in 1775, saw this boundary line emerge on the map of the new world. As can be seen in Figure 1, it extended across a vast expanse of the wilderness from the Ohio River on the north to the Florida peninsula on the south and to the Mississippi River on the west.

Over much of its great length the Southern Indian Boundary Line evolved from a hazy administrative concept, conceived in expediency, to a geographic reality demarcated across the untamed frontier landscape. The remainder of its length was delineated in detail in eighteenth century documents and maps. Needless to say, the Southern Indian Boundary Line was a factor of great moment to the Indians, pioneer settlers, and British administrators concerned with America's first "west" since it was a restrictive barrier beyond which white settlement was not allowed to extend.

For brevity the following points are enumerated in summary without further discussion. They are considerations which seem indispensable in any attempt to bring the Southern Indian Boundary Line out of the obscurity in which it has resided for two centuries.

1. As the struggle for eastern America occupying Europe's three greatest powers came to a head in the middle decades of the eighteenth century, the Indian tribes, armed and informed by the Europeans, played an increasingly pivotal role.

2. As Britain emerged victorious over France and Spain, she realized that her tenure in interior America would depend on an ability to achieve a *modus vivendi* with the powerful Indian tribes living there.

3. The chief cause of discontent and disaffection on the part of the Indians was their fear of losing their hunting grounds and tribal lands to the advancing tide of white colonists from the seaboard.

4. Britain adopted a policy aimed at containing her bourgeoning colonies to the Atlantic slope while guaranteeing the Indian tribes the unmolested possession of the interior.

5. To implement this policy and clearly mark the line of division between King George's white and red subjects, the Southern Indian Boundary Line was painstakingly negotiated, ratified, delineated, and, in a large measure, demarcated.

6. The diligent efforts of John Stuart, His Majesty's Superintendent for Indian Affairs in the southern department, in carrying out the British program resulted in an impressive corpus of manuscript descriptions, surveyor's sketches, and carefully

executed maps which can be effectively employed to reconstruct the Southern Indian Boundary Line.

Surprisingly, there was no published source, be it historical atlas, reference work, scholarly monograph, or paper, to which the investigator of the Southern Indian landscape could turn to find this significant and extensive element reliably illustrated or described. The task was to translate the corpus of manuscript maps, sketches, and descriptions of the Southern Indian Boundary Line to topographic maps of the present day. Regrettably space does not permit a systematic review of all the original maps employed in this cartographic reconstruction.

Rather than attempt any sort of comprehensive review of the many early maps utilized in reconstructing the Southern Indian Boundary, three are reproduced here with brief comments. It is hoped that anthropologists and others will identify ways in which these and similar maps might be employed in reconstructing other facets of the Southern Indian landscape.

Figure 2 is a photographic reproduction of William Bonar's artistically embellished map of the mid-eighteenth century Creek Indian heartland, along the Coosa, Tallapoosa, and Chattahoochee Rivers. The area shown includes that portion of Alabama which stretches from the Coosa, north of Montgomery, south and eastward to the juncture of the Chattahoochee and Flint Rivers in northernmost Florida. Although distance is badly distorted, the map shows the names and locations of many Creek towns as well as two of the chief routes into the area from Georgia and South Carolina. The "French Fort" shown on the Coosa River near the fork of the Alabama (Moville) River was Fort Toulouse, built by the French in 1716. A plan of the fort was included as one of the six vignettes embellishing the margins of the map. The other vignettes include intimate firsthand views of the Creeks, their structures, and implements of peace as well as war.

Bonar accompanied Samuel Pepper, a representative of the governor of South Carolina, on a diplomatic mission to the Creeks during a period of considerable tension. The resourceful Bonar gained access to the French stronghold, Fort Toulouse, in the guise of a packhorseman. He was discovered by the French and arrested. While enroute under guard to the French headquarters at Mobile he was rescued by a party of pro-English Upper Creeks. His map was intended to give the Carolinians a clearer view of the conditions then existing in the Creek heartland. It was recognized as valuable by his con-

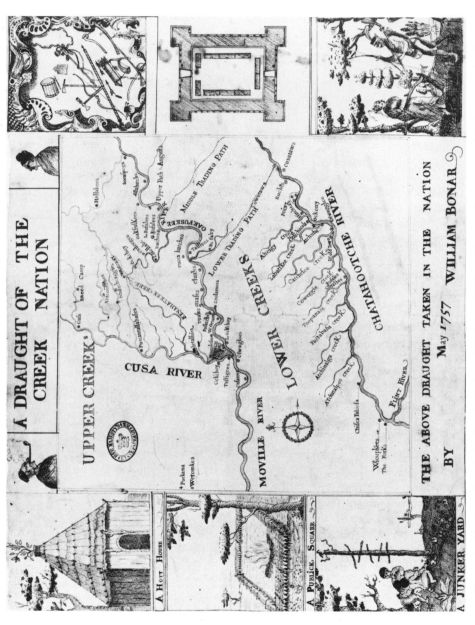

Figure 2. "A Draught of the Creek Nation, 1757," by William Bonar. (From the original manuscript in the British Public Record Office, C.O. 700 Carolina/21. Crown Copyright Material reproduced with permission.)

temporaries and today represents a rich source for anyone studying
the mid-eighteenth century Creek Indian landscape of the Southeast.

Figure 3 is a reproduction of a manuscript draught of the boundary
line which was surveyed between the Cherokee lands and the colony
of South Carolina in 1766. As can be seen it is an official document,
inscribed by the Cherokee representative as well as the Carolina surveyor and commissioner. The line was surveyed from the Savannah
River northeastward for approximately fifty-five miles to the Reedy
River near the crossing of present day state route 101. The map shows
a number of blazed line trees which are identified as to species as well
as several named creeks and rivers. Of particular interest is the pair
of parallel dotted lines which indicate the route of the "Road to Fort
Prince George," the South Carolina outpost in the Lower Cherokee
county. The map is of continuing significance since the surveyed line
it shows still functions as the boundary between Anderson and Abbe-
ville counties in South Carolina.

The last map in this series relating to the reconstruction of the
Southern Indian Boundary Line is Figure 4. For clarity it has been
redrawn from Samuel Savery's original manuscript dated January
1769. The area shown lay along the course of the Georgia-Creek
Indian Boundary Line in the eastern part of the colony. Included are
portions of several present day counties lying along a rough arc about
forty miles to the west of Augusta. It is a valuable and interesting
map, showing as it does the location of the outermost fringe of the
Georgia settlement frontier during the summer of 1768 when Samuel
Savery laboriously conducted his survey and boundary demarcation.
The surveyor's descriptions of the character and quality of the land
near the line are of particular interest. Many of the place names of
creeks and other features shown have changed with time so this map
would be particularly valuable to anyone attempting to interpret
early documentary references or descriptions concerning the area
shown. The "Creek Path" indicated is a segment of one of the most
important aboriginal routeways in the Southeast. It was known as the
Lower Trading Road or Lower Creek Trading Path and crossed the
Ogeechee River near the present day Georgia community of Agricola
(Goff 1953).

ABORIGINAL FOREST COVER IN GREENE COUNTY GEORGIA—A LARGE SCALE STUDY

In addition to the many hundreds of small and medium scale manuscript maps listed and described by Cumming in his book, *The South-*

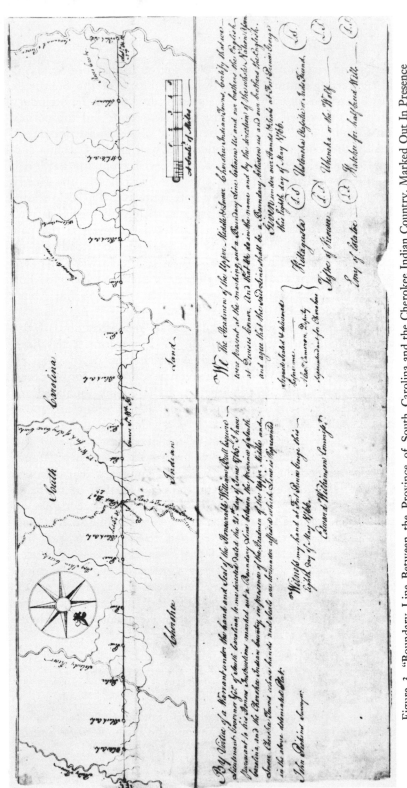

Figure 3. "Boundary Line Between the Province of South Carolina and the Cherokee Indian Country, Marked Out In Presence of the Head Men of the Upper, Middle and Lower Cherokee Towns, Whose Hands and Seals are Affixed. . .," by John Pickens. 1776. (From the original manuscript in the British Public Record Office, C.O. 700 Carolina/26. Crown Copyright Material, reproduced with permission.)

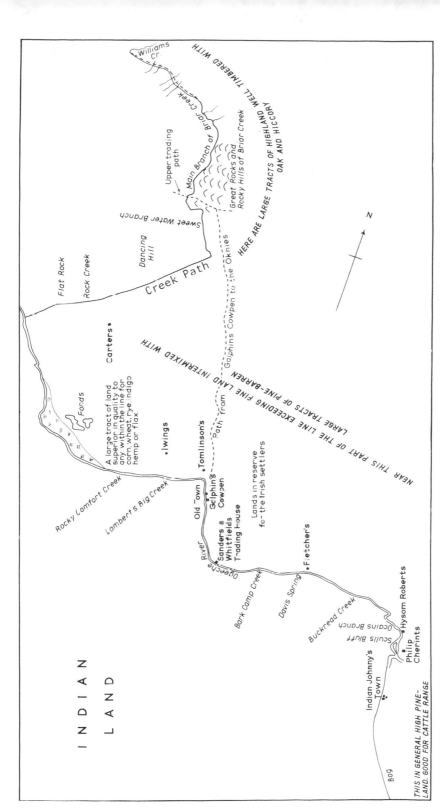

Figure 4. Tracing from Samuel Savery's map of the Georgia-Creek boundary of 1768. (British Public Record Office, C.O. 700 Georgia/14. Crown Copyright Material, reproduced with permission.)

east In Early Maps, there exisits another vast body of primary cartographic evidence which may be valuably employed in efforts to
reconstruct past Southern Indian landscapes. This is composed of the
several million large scale land maps, called plats, which were prepared as the public domain of the eastern colonies and states was delivered from governmental control into the hands of private citizens
and commercial enterprise. This vast corpus of primary evidence is
almost untapped at the present time. Its potential value seems
enormous.

As might be imagined, the transfer of land, the most fundamental
and prized resource of the age, was highly formalized and generally
required that an accurate survey and description of the transferred
land parcel be prepared and recorded in a central administrative office.
The importance of these plats and documents has resulted in their
careful preservation to the present day in our state and national
archives. The surveyor general of Georgia, for example, maintains
approximately one and one-half million survey plats and documents
which are available for study and scholarly use.

Figure 5 is a copy made from a particularly interesting survey
plat found in the Georgia archives. Thanks to the doodling of one
early land surveyor, this plat presents a contemporary view of an
eighteenth century land surveying party at work. The surveyor can
be seen in frock coat and breeches, sighting on a black oak corner
tree through the sight vanes of his circumferentor or surveyor's
compass mounted on its "jacobs staff." The chain carriers, following
him along his traverse, are shown wearing bits of their Revolutionary
War army uniforms. These Revolutionary veterans are measuring
distance with a Gunter's chain composed of carefully measured wire
links. Edmund Gunter perfected this measuring device in 1620. It
was based on the statute rod as a unit of land measurement with 100
links which equalled 66 feet or one rod. Still another member of the
party is shown aiming at a deer with a flintlock.

It can be seen that the surveyors noted many landscape features
on their plats. These often included such things as tree types, drainage
features, soil quality, notable terrain features such as hills, large
rocks, swamps, and springs. Many plats showed aboriginal cultural
features such as Indian burial and temple mounds, paths, old fields,
and villages, as well as fishing and hunting camps. There can be little
doubt that these plats may be employed to yield valuable data concerning the landscape of the Southeast on the eve of its occupation
by sedentary European cultivators.

Again, rather than describing and discussing the original land

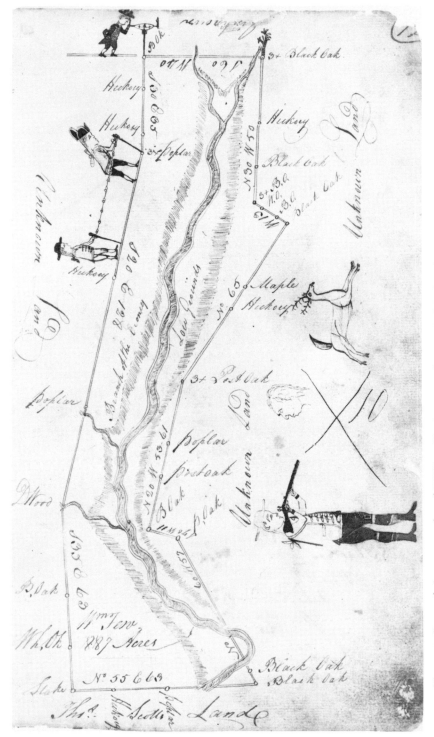

Figure 5. Copy of the survey plat of William Few's grant of 1784, (original scale, 1 inch represents 20 chains). This plat is one of many thousands maintained by the Georgia Surveyor General's Department, reproduced here with permission.

survey plats in general terms only, it seems advisable at this point to demonstrate their value in a more specific way through a large scale study which made use of them. This study is a small portion of a larger effort to gain a clearer and more accurate understanding of the character and composition of the forest cover of eastern America in the late eighteenth century.

Even a superficial examination of the accounts written by early explorers and travelers in the Southeast reveals a view of the forests which is widely at variance with what the present landscape reveals. One of these early travelers through the aboriginal Southeastern forests and glades was the well known Pennsylvania naturalist William Bartram (1958).

Bartram's writings have been extensively utilized by scholars interested in the eighteenth century South. Doubts have arisen from time to time, however, concerning his accuracy as a reporter of the aboriginal southern scene. Who, for example, would not have second thoughts regarding his colorful description of the hardwood dominated forest cover of the area now included in Georgia's Greene and Oglethorpe counties, if they were only familiar with the present day pine dominated scene in the area?

Bartram traveled through this portion of Georgia during the spring of 1773. He was almost rhapsodic in his glowing description of the forest he observed there. He wrote of "the most magnificent forest I had ever seen." He went on to describe

> this sublime forest; the ground perfectly a level green plain, thinly planted by nature with the most stately forest trees, such as the gigantic black oak . . . whose mighty trunks seemingly of an equal height, appeared like superb columns. To keep within the bounds of truth and reality, in describing the magnitude and grandeur of these trees, would, I fear, fail of credibility; yet I think I can assert, that many of the black oaks measured eight, nine, ten, and eleven feet diameter five feet above ground, as we measured several that were above thirty feet girt, and from hence they ascend perfectly strait, with a gradual taper, forty or fifty feet to the limbs (1958:24).

In an effort to check Bartram's description of the aboriginal hardwood dominated forest in Greene and Oglethorpe counties, original survey plats were employed as a source of data for a partial reconstruction.

The original survey plats for the study area, shown in Figure 6, were retrieved from Georgia State Surveyor General's files. The

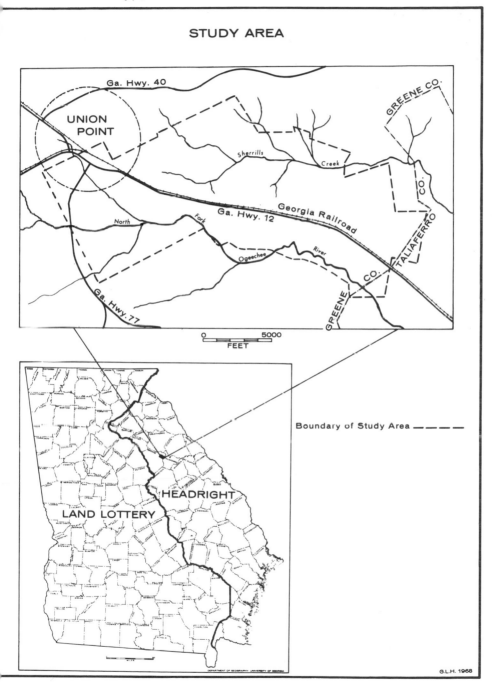

Figure 6. Location Maps Showing the Study Area in Greene County, Georgia.
(From an original by Gerald L. Holder.)

several plats covering this area were then mosaicked jigsaw-puzzle fashion. With the aid of a Saltzman projector this mosaic was then keyed to a topographic map of the area. This operation was necessary since the study area is within the Headright region of Georgia and so lacks any regulated cadastral system such as that present in the western two thirds of the state. With the study area correctly located on the map and landscape of the present day, attention was turned to the forest cover (Holder 1968).

It will be recalled that land surveying practices in the eighteenth century entailed the identification, as to species, of several line, corner, and witness trees on each plat registered. In addition to this data, a number of the plats included the surveyor's descriptive commentary on the general character of the forest cover, as he perceived it, on the land surveyed. In all cases where such verbal descriptions appeared they emphasized the hardwoods, oak and hickory, and only occasionally was pine included. When pine did occur it followed oak and hickory. After noting these verbal descriptions, the plats were then scrutinized more closely and the individual tree types were counted. A total of 197 trees were identified on the mosaicked plats of the study area. Of these, 80% were hardwoods with oaks alone accounting for 57% of the total number. Only 18% of the identified trees were pines. A check of recent aerial photography of the study area revealed that hardwoods account for only about 40% of the cover with pines accounting for 60% of the total.

It would seem that the original plats have lent confirmation to William Bartram's account of a hardwood dominant forest in this portion of the eighteenth century Georgia Piedmont. The plats are, however, only one source of data and represent a somewhat biased sample of what the original forest was really like. They are biased because surveyors probably tended to select a hardwood tree on which to strike a blaze rather than a less durable pine, if the choice was available. This fact probably resulted in the inclusion of a higher percentage of hardwoods than a random sample would have produced.

Other data such as maps, documentary accounts, saw mill ledgers, the timbers found in extant old buildings, and pollen grain counts in marshy beds need to be considered before definite conclusions can be framed concerning the forest cover of the study area two centuries ago. It does seem clear, however, that this source of data confirms rather than denies Bartram's accuracy as a reporter of the eighteenth century scene.

CONCLUSION

Anthropologists and geographers share a large common ground in both the material which they examine and the methodology of that examination. In this paper a small part of that common ground has been uncovered through the examination and analysis of early maps of the South. The small and large scale studies discussed here are of limited interest in themselves. What is of major interest, however, is the fact that these early maps represent poorly understood and neglected data sources which may contribute to a deeper understanding of the South's aboriginal heritage. The maps also represent an area of research effort where the expertise of the geographer can valuably contribute to the goals of the anthropologist and vice versa. Perhaps they chart the way toward that fusion of the disciplines to which Sauer alluded so long ago.

REFERENCES

Bartram, William, 1958. *Travels Through North and South Carolina, Georgia, East and West Florida* . . . . Naturalist's Edition, Francis Harper, ed. (New Haven: Yale University Press).

Broek, Jan O. M. 1932. *The Santa Clara Valley, California: A Study in Landscape Changes* (Utrecht: N.V.A. Oosthoek's Uitgevers).

————— 1965. *Geography: Its Scope and Spirit* (Columbus: Charles E. Merrill).

Coppock, J. T. 1968. Maps As Sources For the Study of Land Use in the Past. *Imago Mundi* 22:37-49.

Cumming, William P. 1962. *The Southeast In Early Maps* (Chapel Hill: University of North Carolina Press).

————— 1966. Mapping of the Southeast: The First Two Centuries. *The Southeastern Geographer* 6:3-19.

De Vorsey, Louis, Jr., 1966a. The Colonial Southeast On "An Accurate General Map." *The Southeastern Geographer* 6:20-32.

—————, 1966b. *The Indian Boundary In The Southern Colonies, 1763-1775* (Chapel Hill: The University of North Carolina Press).

Frake, Charles O., 1962. Cultural Ecology and Ethnography. *American Anthropologist* 64:53-59.

Friis, Herman R., 1966. Highlights of the Geographical and Cartographical Activities of the Federal Government In the Southeastern United States: 1776-1865. *The Southeastern Geographer* 6:41-57.

Goff, John H., 1953. Some Major Indian Trading Paths Across the Georgia Piedmont. *Georgia Mineral News Letter* 6:122-131.

Harley, J. B., 1968. The Evaluation of Early Maps: Towards a Methodology. *Imago Mundi* 22:62-74.

Holder, Gerald L., 1968. Landholdings Along the North Fork of the Ogeechee River in 1786. Unpublished Seminar Paper, Department of Geography, University of Georgia.

Koeman, C., 1968. Levels of Historical Evidence in Early Maps (With Examples). *Imago Mundi* 22:75-80.

Mikesell, Marvin W., 1967. Geographic Perspectives In Anthropology. *Annals of the Association of American Geographers* 57:617-634.

Newcomb, Robert M., 1969. Twelve Working Approaches to Historical Geography. *Yearbook of the Association of Pacific Coast Georgraphers* 31:27-50.

Ristow, Walter W., 1966. State Maps of the Southeast to 1833. *The Southeastern Geographer* 6:33-40.

Sauer, Carl O., 1963. *Land and Life: A Selection From the Writings of Carl Ortwin Sauer*, John Leighley, ed. (Berkeley and Los Angeles: University of California Press).

Skelton, R. A., 1965. *Looking At An Early Map* (Lawrence: University of Kansas Libraries).

Physical Anthropology of Indians of the Old South

William S. Pollitzer

In a sense the physical anthropology of the Indians of the South begins with the earliest observations of the European adventurers who travelled among them, trading and surveying, and recording the appearance of body and face. Thus, Lawson (1714) not only speaks of the stature of the natives of North Carolina, of their tawny color and their scant facial hair, but also of the deformation of the skull induced by the cradleboard—an early reminder of the influence of culture upon physique and a caution to all subsequent students of skulls. Subsequent to that early contact we have the impressions also of Adair, Bartram, Swan, and many others (Swanton 1946). Swanton's extensive studies of Southern Indians rest largely upon voluminous historical documents, and they understandably contain relatively little detailed account of physical measurements. Boas published on the physical anthropology of the Indians of North America as early as 1895, including measurements on stature and cephalic index among Cherokees, Choctaws, Chickasaws, and Creeks (Boas 1895). In the last decade of the nineteenth century and the first two decades of the twentieth, Clarence B. Moore excavated many sites in the South, sometimes finding and describing skeletal material.

Large scale descriptions of the bones of the dead begin with Hrdlička. In his study of the Lenape or Delawares (Hrdlička 1916), based on 57 skeletons from Mausee near the junction of New York, New Jersey, and Pennsylvania, he characterized these Algonkian people as having good-sized skulls which were oval to elliptical in shape and moderate in length; he found them similar to Iroquois, and different from eastern round-heads. In a subsequent publication (Hrdlička 1927) he reported on similar Algonkian remains from Maryland, Virginia, and Kentucky whose mean cephalic index ranged

31

from 74 to 77, with a high vault and a medium to large face. In his "Indians of the Gulf States" (Hrdlička 1940) he catalogued skulls from many locations in the South, and especially from Florida; on the basis of the almost universal distribution of these broad-heads, he recognized the "Gulf type."

But these early classifications could not take into account the complex relationships between populations and their temporal sequence; it is the work of the modern archeologist which has added the dimension of time to that of space. When Funkhouser (1938) described the osteological material from the Norris Basin in eastern Tennessee, he found the people to be tall, of slight and graceful build, with round heads and broad faces, and considered them as probably of the same stock as those to the north and west in the Mississippi Valley. Skårland (1939) examined the remains from the Chiggerville site in Kentucky and described a population with long, high heads and short faces. When Newman and Snow (1942) investigated the skeletal material from Pickwick Basin near the junction of Alabama, Mississippi, and Tennessee, they differentiated the early, undeformed long heads with high vaults and greater tooth wear of the Shell Mounds from the later, deformed round heads of Koger's Island.

Using Pearson's Coefficient of Racial Likeness, von Bonin and Morant (1938) sought a statistical classification of the Indians based on the series of skulls known at that time. The similarity of the Florida remains to those of California they regarded as in conformity with those peripheral populations that von Eickstedt called "Margids." But they were compelled to separate their Kentucky skulls from Hrdlička's Algonkians on the basis of metrical distinctions. In 1948 Snow gave a thorough report on these abundant Indian Knoll skeletons, dating from the Archaic period. Of 1234 individuals, 521 were measurable, including 475 skulls. These short people had small, ovoid skulls with high vaults and a cranial index averaging 76, and large faces with prominent cheek-bones. One-fourth of them showed signs of flattening at the front of the head and a very few showed flattening at the rear of the head as well. Originally considered dating from the early Christian era they are now generally recognized as being at least 5000 years old. This gold mine of osteology has been reworked since, with studies of long bones being reported as recently as 1968 (Graham and Yarbrough).

Lewis and Kneberg (1961) believe that the people of their Eva Site in Tennessee represent a similar archaic population extending from 6000 to 4000 B.C. Of the 49 measurable skulls, a third are long-headed, only 11% are round-headed, while the majority are intermediate. Further indication of their similarity to the Indian Knoll people is found in their high vault.

When Georg Neumann examined the skeletal remains from Keyauwee in North Carolina (Neumann n. d.), he considered these Catawban people similar to those of Indian Knoll. On the basis of these and other finds he defined the Iswanid variety, the term itself derived from the Catawba word meaning "people of the river." They are characterized by a small, moderately long, ovoid skull with small to medium brow ridges and medium frontal slope. The face is moderate in all proportions and has pronounced lateral zygomatic projection. Neumann believes this variety is represented in the Shell Mound series of Pickwick Basin, in the Chiggerville site, and possibly in sites as widely separated as southern New England and Florida. He sees similarities between the Iswanid and the Basket Makers of the southwestern United States.

In Neumann's scheme the Walcolids are roughly equivalent to Hrdlička's Gulf type or von Eickstedt's Centralids, best represented by the series from the Spoon River focus from Central Illinois. The skull is large, intermediate in length, ovoid, and high, with medium brow ridges and medium to slight frontal slope. The face is largish, rugged, and moderately long. When Snow (1945) described the skeletal remains from the Tchefuncte site on the lower Mississippi, he noted that their skulls were high-vaulted and moderately rounded, that their faces were broad, and that their stature was medium; he saw a closer relationship of them to the early Shell Mound people than to the later Koger's Island people; and he considered them a possible admixture of early longheads and later round-heads. Collins (1941) studied skeletal remains from Copell Place, a Tchefuncte site on Pecan Island, Louisiana, and considered the people a variant of the Indian Knoll group. Neumann thinks that the Tchefuncte population may possibly be Walcolid.

The important Woodland site of Adena in the Ohio River valley was reported by Webb and Snow (1945). They contrast these round-headed people with massive flat faces and broad high foreheads and extensive occipital flattening with the Indian Knollers. Neumann thinks they may have provided a link with the southern Walcolids. Hertzberg has described a series of skeletal material from Ricketts Mound (1940a) and another from the nearby Wright site (1940b) which may also fall into this category. Their large heads are quite broad and with long faces, and the long bones indicate a people of medium stature. More recent excavations in Florida (Jennings, et al. 1957) have revealed further remains from the Woodland stage that fit best into Neumann's Walcolid variety also.

In Neumann's terminology the Algonkians of the East are the Lenapids who entered the archeological scene late and continued into the historic period. Their large, ovoid skulls tend toward long-headedness with brow ridges and signs of muscularity; the face is moderately long and rugged with medium prognathism.

The burials at Hiwassee Island in Tennessee, described by Lewis and Kneberg (1946) include three components which appear to extend from late Mississippian into historic times. The appreciable variability in skulls, especially among the later burials, suggests to the authors admixture of several peoples, although those of the middle or Dallas focus are thought to be primarily Creeks. Deformation, absent in the earliest skulls, is evident in several of the later ones.

Woodland and Mississippian traits were noted in the Peachtree site, whose skeletal remains were reported by Stewart (1941). Located in western North Carolina near historic Cherokee towns, it is possible that that tribe may have been among its occupants. Of 39 individuals, 16 showed cranial deformity, 14 did not, and 9 were too incomplete for information; cranial form was reported as variable.

Hulse (1941) has provided us with a neat analysis of the people who lived at Irene in Chatham County, Georgia, almost into the historic period. Of medium to submedium stature, the people are essentially round-headed but quite variable. Hulse argues that they may show two genetic strains, chiefly on the basis of a peculiar bun-shaped occiput. As is so often the case with later Indians, some cranial deformation shows in one-third of the skulls.

The Stalling's Island Mound, near Augusta, Georgia, has provided information on people who lived into the historic period. Round-headedness, but not usually cranial deformation, is the rule among the poorly preserved skulls from this site (Claflin 1931). Cottier and Dickens (1965) have written of remains of skeletons, also not well preserved, from the Shine Mound Site in Alabama, which apparently extends almost into the historic period.

Near the beginning of the historic period in Virginia are the skeletal remains from the Tolliferro and Clarksville sites in the Kerr Reservoir Basin on the Roanoke River, reported by St. Hoyme and Bass (1962). These two sites were evidently occupied by Occaneechi Indians from about 1500 to 1600 (or earlier) and from 1600 to 1675, respectively. The authors indicate that the Tolliferro crania fit well with such southeastern material as Indian Knoll and Shell Mound. While the Clarksville population are similar, they are more round-headed and somewhat larger. Related material from Mecklenberg, Virginia, measured and described by Sigmon (1963), shows evidence of appreciable admixture. Phelps measured related Tutelo people from Yadkin and Occaneechi from Alamance, both in North Carolina (Pollitzer et al. 1967).

In the Carolinas and Virginia, the Siouan people, of slight frame and small delicate skulls of intermediate shape, were found in the proto-historic period between the tall, long-headed coastal Algonkians and the more rugged, angular, round-headed people near the mountains. The latter, including both the Iroquois-speaking Cherokee and the Muskogean-speaking inhabitants of Town Creek would fall into Neumann's Walcolid variety. The relationship of several of these populations to the living Catawba, survivors of a Siouan-speaking people of the East, will be described presently.

The physical anthropologist is interested in the abnormal as well as the normal variations, and the bones and teeth have provided an opportunity for the study of pathology. Thus, Funkhouser (1938) reported on poor teeth and on bone disease from the Norris Basin; Newman and Snow (1942) noted considerable arthritis at Pickwick Basin; Snow (1948) noted the lumbar arthritis of the Indian Knoll remains and the osteoporosis and osteitis in the Tchefuncte people (1945); Stewart (1941) noted ear exostoses and osteitis at the Peachtree site; Hulse (1941) reported dental and skeletal anomalies from Irene; Sigmon (1963) wrote of caries and other possible disease; and St. Hoyme and Bass (1962) described the pathology of their Roanoke River sites. Stewart, who called attention to possible pre-Columbian syphilis earlier (1941), has revived interest with his recent report on lesions of the frontal bone (Stewart and Quade 1969), some of which appear to be syphilitic in origin, in Indians of the Archaic in several locations including southern ones.

Mehta (1969) studied the dentition of the Shell Mound Indians of Alabama to test the association of malocculusion and attrition. While the tooth wear was excessive he found crowding in only 29 of 636 teeth studied. In 23 skulls from the site, three had slight and one had moderate overbite. Investigation of Arkansas skulls (Mehta and Evans 1966) revealed similar results which suggest that attrition and malocclusion do not go together.

We must not fall into the habit of thinking that new skulls are produced by the mating of two previous skulls. Our ultimate concern is with the entire organism. Hill (1963) has recently provided us with a detailed dissection of a Cherokee Indian, which he found to be not especially "Mongoloid" in his anatomy.

Few anthropometric studies of living Indians of the South have been done, but Krogman's very thorough monograph on the Seminoles of Oklahoma, derived from the South, is an approximation. From genealogies and measurements he found (Krogman 1935) considerable evidence of admixture of the Seminoles with other Indian groups, especially the neighboring Creeks, and some with non-Indian peoples as well.

How much of the change noted in Indian populations with time is due to displacement of one population by another and how much is evolutionary change? M. Newman (1962) recently addressed himself to this question, examining head form and stature. Citing especially the data from northern Alabama, he believes an increase of 4 or 5 cms. over 5000 years among Indians of the Southeast is an evolutionary change which may be related to climate, perhaps also to nutrition and health, and influenced only slightly by the interbreeding of different populations. He also finds the brachycephalization, the tendency to broader heads, as shown by an increase of six index points over this span of time, further indication of evolutionary change. He would recognize only two major migrations of Indians into America, with subsequent evolution of varieties occurring on this continent. Neumann (1960) apparently accepts the evolution of the Walcolid variety along with the development of the middle Mississippi culture phase.

To understand better the relationships between populations, anthropologists have turned toward those traits with known, precise genetic mechanisms and have attempted to characterize groups by their "gene pools." As races may be viewed as interbreeding populations who share the same genes, an attempt has been made to characterize groups by the frequency of various readily determined traits, such as the blood types, governed by single genes. A large and growing battery of inherited factors of blood are now applicable among the living for a study of their migrations and relationships. One new hemoglobin, $G_{Coushatta}$, was discovered in the Alabama Coushatta Indians on their reservation in east Texas where these Muskogean tribes have lived since about 1800 (Schneider et al. 1964). In this hemoglobin, glutamine replaces alanine in the beta chain (Bowman et al. 1967). Haptoglobins have also been studied among the Alabama Coushatta Indians; their Hp^1 gene frequency of 0.37 is similar to that of most other American Indians (Shim and Bearn 1964).

Cerumen (earwax) can generally be classified into two types that are genetically controlled; the dry variety is dominant over the wet.

Study of 432 Choctaw Indians of Mississippi revealed 21% of the dry type, a lower percentage than that in most western tribes (Martin and Jackson 1969). Investigation among the Seminoles of Florida showed 48% of the dry variety (Hirschhorn 1970).

While the genetics of dermatoglyphics is not fully understood, a well recognized hereditary component in such palm prints permits them to be used in a fashion similar to that of the monogenic traits. Rife (1968) found the pattern of the Seminoles to be similar to those of most other North American Indians, and differences on the three reservations reflect their known genetic relationship.

Our blood type survey of the Cherokee Indians on their reservation in western North Carolina (Pollitzer et al. 1962) provided an opportunity to compare genetically the remnant of this once powerful and flourishing tribe with other Indian populations. In their blood factors, including the high frequency of Group O, of M, and of Rh positive, and their absence of abnormal hemoglobin, they are similar to most other American Indian tribes. The Diego factor found in many other Indian groups was absent, and Rh[1] was more common than in most other Indians studied. The study bore out the conclusion of Glass (1955) that the Indian contributed relatively little to the gene pool of the Negro in America. Gene flow from Negro into Indian, however, is a different question for which our study provides no definitive answers. In our sample the only indication of Negro admixture came from one case each of Hunter and of Henshaw blood types, usually associated with African populations. The absence of Rh_0, J_s, S^u, and V blood types and hemoglobin S argue against appreciable Negroid admixture.

Ample opportunities for Negro-Indian admixture in the Old South existed. In earliest colonial days some white owners worked Negro and Indian slaves on the same plantation; runaway Negroes often took refuge among Indian tribes; and Indians themselves sometimes had Negro slaves. Thus, a census report of the Cherokee population in 1835 listed 16,542 Cherokee Indians, 1592 Negro slaves, and 201 whites who had married into the tribe. While matings among all three major groups undoubtedly occurred, our blood type data suggest that the "mixed-bloods" among the Eastern Cherokees are predominantly mixed with whites, probably with the English and Scotch-Irish who prevailed on the frontier. Indeed, the proportion of Indian ancestry estimated by gene frequencies in the "mixed-bloods" on the assumption of admixture with an English stock is almost identical to the 62% actually found. Many of the offspring of Negro-Indian unions evidently went westward in the great forced migration of 1838, while some others remained in small communities bordering the Cherokee reservation.

The Seminole Indians of Florida (Pollitzer et al. 1970) provide a different story, in some ways parallel to the Cherokees and in some ways strikingly different. Like the Cherokees they came into continuing conflict with the need and greed of the white men, and many of their numbers were forcibly removed to Oklahoma on the "Trail of Tears." But whereas the territory and overlordship of the Cherokee was vast at the time of European contact and declined almost to a vanishing point by the mid-nineteenth century, the Seminoles grew by gradual accretion from the early eighteenth century onward as Indians from Georgia, mostly Creek with some Yemassee and Yuchi, moved into Florida and in time successfully challenged the power of the United States in two wars. The Oconee, who had settled at Alachua in north central Florida by 1750, became the Cow Creek Indians and the forerunners of the Seminoles now at Brighton on the north shore of Lake Okeechobee. Related Indians settled around Lake Miccosukee in northwestern Florida, the forerunners of the present-day Big Cypress community bordering the Everglades and the related population at Dania. From the start the lives of these Indians were intertwined with Negroes who joined them, sometimes as slaves and sometimes as free allies.

Our study of the Seminoles in Florida included both physical measurements and blood studies. These Indians are quite variable but most often of copper coloring, moderately tall, round-headed, and intermediate in nose and face dimensions. In blood factors, the very high incidence of Group O, of Rh positive, and of M puts them in line with most other Indian populations. Like the Cherokees they lack Rh_o, but unlike the Cherokees they possess Diego. The presence of hemoglobin S and of G-6-P-D variants is indicative of some Negroid admixture. In general, the distribution of both the physical measurements and the serological factors on the reservations at Brighton on the one hand and at Big Cypress and Dania on the other bears out the historical relationship between the two populations. Moreover, both methods of study agree that the Seminoles are predominantly Indian, with some admixture from both whites and Negroes.

In our research on the Catawba Indians near Rock Hill, South Carolina, we were able to make some estimate of their relationship not only to other present-day populations but also to Indians of the past. During the climactic phase in North Carolina, such Siouan tribes as the Catawba, Saponi, and Tutelo lived along the rivers of the Piedmont. In this proto-historic period the Catawba evidently lost their earlier Uwharrie ceramic traits to a Lamar influence from Georgia, like that of the people at Irene, while a distinctive Muskogean people, bearing the PeeDee culture, had pushed up the river of that name as far as the narrows of the Yadkin (Coe 1952). At the early historic era, some Occaneechi moved on to the Clarksville area from Piedmont Carolina, where their skeletal remains suggest admixture, some of it possibly non-Indian. In time the Catawba moved into South Carolina and absorbed remnants of related Indian tribes. In colonial times they were allied with the English against the Iroquois-speaking tribes. In 1763 they were granted a reservation 15 miles square in York and Lancaster counties, South Carolina. In area, in population, and in the amenities of life, this reserve was steadily reduced in the succeeding years.

In 1962, when the Indians terminated their reservation status, we obtained physical measurements and blood studies (Pollitzer et al. 1967). The serological traits show most clearly that the present-day Catawba are actually about half-Indian and half-white with no significant Negroid admixture. The appearance and the physical measurements, while not as conclusive, are consistent with this estimate, a phenomenon probably due to the influence of the Mormon religion to which they became converted in the late nineteenth century. The Mormons taught that Indians, while not as elevated as whites, could someday become a "white and delightsome people."

In comparing the living Catawba with skeletal populations, appropriate corrections were made for soft parts. In many of their measurements and indices the present-day Catawba still show similarity to remains of the long extinct Indians of the region. The D^2 or distance measure designed by Mahalanobis takes into account both the difference between the means of traits in two or more populations and the intercorrelations between the traits. By this test, they are most similar to the Tutelo of the Yadkin, and next to the people from Indian Knoll and Clarksville. The Occaneechi at Tolliferro are not far removed, while the mixed population from Mecklenberg is most distant.

Although the attempt at blood typing ancient skeletal remains is a dubious procedure, it is noteworthy that our results on bones of 26 individuals of the Yadkin River sites typed by inhibition techniques show that all except two are in Group O and those two are in Group A—much in line with present Indian populations of the area.

Throughout colonial times population pressures led both to migration of Indian tribes and to their gradual absorption into the expanding white culture. While records are understandably hazy, we have evidence of unions of individual Indians, whites, and Negroes, sometimes "free persons of color." Price (1950) has abundantly documented the formation of such triracial isolates in the Southeast, and Berry (1963) has painted a sympathetic portrait of the "mestizo" who has survived into the present-day. Our own studies of the Lumbee (Pollitzer et al. 1964) and the Haliwa, both in North Carolina (Pollitzer et al. 1966), and of the Melungeons of Tennessee and Virginia (Pollitzer and Brown 1969) bear witness to the survival of Indian strains in these biologic and cultural isolates. The last study also suggests their present-day dissolution.

What are the needs for the future study of the physical anthropology of the Indians of the South? One necessary task is the thorough morphological and metrical analysis of osteological material sequestered in our museums not yet studied and reported. This study must take account of the most recent dating of the material and all relevant data contributed by the archeologist, and previous studies should be adjusted accordingly. But classification alone is not enough. We need more understanding of the nature of morphological change, its rate, and its determinants. We must in time come to understand the people in terms of the selective pressures of the environment, of the demographic variables of fertility and mortality, and the nature of health and disease. We need to compare populations not only within the South but with related ones elsewhere and to contrast them with peoples living under quite different conditions. We must reach out to the historian, ethnographer, linguist, and archeologist on the one hand, and toward the biomedical scientists on the other, to make one unified, yet dynamic, picture of the life of the Indians of the South.

REFERENCES

Berry, Brewton, 1963. *Almost White* (New York: Macmillan Co).
Blackwell, R. Q., I-H. Ro, C-S. Liu, H-J. Yang, C-C. Wang, and J.T-H. Huang, 1969. Hemoglobin Variant Found in Koreans, Chinese, and North American Indians. *American Journal of Physical Anthropology* 30:389-392.
Boas, Franz, 1895. Zur Anthropologie der Nordamerikanischen. *Zeitschrift für Ethnologie* 27:366-411.
Bowman, B. H., D. R. Barnett, and R. Hite, 1967. Hemoglobin G_{Coushatta}: a Beta Variant with a Delta-like Substitution. *Biochemistry and Biophysics Research Communication* 26:466-470.
Claflin, W. H., 1931. The Stalling's Island Mound, Columbia County, Georgia. *Papers of the Peabody Museum of American Archeology and Ethnology*, XIV, No. 1 (Cambridge, Mass.: Harvard University Press).

Coe,   Joffre, 1952. The Cultural Sequence of the Carolina Piedmont. In *Archeology of Eastern United States,* J. B. Griffin, ed. (Chicago: University of Chicago Press).

Collins, Henry B. Jr., 1941. Relationships of an Early Indian Cranial Series from Louisiana. *Journal of the Washington Academy of Science* 31:145-155.

Cottier, J. W., and R. S. Dickens, 1965. Preliminary Report on the Skeletal Remains from the Shine Mound Site, Montgomery County, Alabama. Unpublished manuscript, University of Alabama.

Funkhouser, W. D., 1938. A Study of the Physical Anthropology and Pathology of the Osteological Material from the Norris Basin. In *An Archeological Survey of the Norris Basin in Eastern Tennessee,* W. S. Webb, ed., *Bureau of American Ethnology Bulletin* 118. (Washington, D.C.: GPO), pp. 225-251.

Glass, Bentley, 1955. On the Unlikelihood of Significant Admixture of Genes from the North American Indians in the Present Composition of the Negroes of the United States. *American Journal of Human Genetics* 7:368-385.

Graham, T. M., and J. D. Yarbrough, 1968. Anthropometric Studies of the Long Bones of the "Shell Mound" Indians. *American Journal of Physical Anthropology* 28:85-92.

Hertzberg, H. T. E., 1940a. The Skeletal Remains from Ricketts Mound (site 3, Montgomery County). *University of Kentucky Reports in Anthropology and Archeology,* 3: (6) (University of Kentucky Press), pp. 233-257.

————————————, 1940b. Skeletal Material from the Wright Site, Montgomery County. In the Wright Mounds, Sites 6 and 7. *University of Kentucky Reports in Anthropology,* 5: (1) (University of Kentucky Press), pp. 83-102.

Hill, W. C. Osman, 1963. The Soft Anatomy of a North American Indian. *American Journal of Physical Anthropology* 21:245-269.

Hirschhorn, H. H., 1970. Cerumen Types and PTC-Tasting in the Seminole Indians of Florida. *American Journal of Physical Anthropology* 33:107-108.

Hrdlička, Ales, 1916. Physical Anthropology of the Lenape or Delawares and of the Eastern Indians in General. *Bureau of American Ethnology Bulletin,* 62 (Washington, D.C.: GPO).

————————————, 1927. Catalogue of Human Crania in the U. S. National Museum Collection; the Algonkian and Related Iroquois; Siouan, Caddoan, Salish and Sahaptin, Shoshonean and California Indians. *Proceedings of the U. S. National Museum,* 69, art. 5 (Washington, D. C.: GPO).

————————————, 1940. Catalogue of Human Crania in the U. S. National Museum: Indians of the Gulf States. *Proceedings of the U. S. National Museum,* 87 (Washington, D.C.: GPO), pp. 315-464.

Hulse, Frederick, 1941. The People who Lived at Irene: Physical Anthropology. In *Irene Mound Site, Chatham County, Georgia,* Joseph Caldwell and Catherine McCann, eds. (Athens: The University of Georgia Press).

Jennings, J. D., G. R. Willey, and M. T. Newman, 1957. The Ormond Beach Mound, East Central Florida. *Bureau of American Ethnology Bulletin,* 164 (Washington, D.C.: GPO), pp. 1-85.

Krogman, W. M., 1935. *The Physical Anthropology of the Seminole Indians of Oklahoma.* Comitato Italiano Per Lo Studio Dei Problem, Della Popolazione, Series III, Vol. II (Roma: Tipografia Failli).

Lawson, John, 1714. *History of North Carolina* (Richmond, Va.: Garrett and Massey).

Lewis, T.M.N., and M. Kneberg, 1946. *Hiwassee Island* (Knoxville: University of Tennessee Press).

————————————, 1961. *Eva, An Archaic Site* (Knoxville: University of Tennessee Press).

Martin, L. M., and J. F. Jackson, 1969. Cerumen Types in Choctaw Indians. *Science* 163:677-678.

Mehta, J. D., 1969. A Comparative Study of the Dentition of the Shell Mound Indians of Alabama. *Alabama Journal of Medicine Science* 6:208-212.

Mehta, J. D., and C. C. Evans, 1966. A study of Attrition of Teeth in the Arkansas Indian Skulls. *Angle Orthodontist* 36:248-257.

Neumann, Georg K., n.d. The Skeletal Remains from Keyauwee. Unpublished manuscript in the Research Laboratories of Anthropology (Chapel Hill, University of N.C.).

------------------------------------, 1952. Archeology and Race in the American Indian. In *Archeology of Eastern United States*, J. B. Griffin, ed. (Chicago: University of Chicago Press).

------------------------------------, 1960. Origins of the Indians of the Middle Mississippi Area. *Proceedings of the Indiana Academy of Science* 69:66-68.

Newman, M. T., 1962. Evolutionary Changes in Body Size and Head Form in American Indians. *American Anthropologist* 64:237-257.

Newman, M. T., and C. E. Snow, 1942. Preliminary Report on the Skeletal Material from Pickwick Basin, Alabama. In *An Archeological Survey of Pickwick Basin in the Adjacent Portions of the States of Alabama, Mississippi, and Tennessee*, W. S. Webb and D. L. DeJarnette, eds. *Bureau of American Ethnology Bulletin*, 129 (Washington, D.C.: GPO), pp. 393-507.

Pollitzer, W. S., R. C. Hartmann, H. Moore, R. E. Rosenfield, H. Smith, S. Hakim, P. J. Schmidt, and W. C. Leyshon, 1962. Blood Types of the Cherokee Indians. *American Journal of Physical Anthropology* 20:33-43.

Pollitzer, W. S., 1964. Analysis of a Tri-racial Isolate. *Human Biology* 36:362-373.

Pollitzer, W. S., R. M. Menegaz-Bock, and J. C. Herion, 1966. Factors in the Microevolution of a Triracial Isolate. *American Journal of Human Genetics* 18:26-38.

Pollitzer, W. S., D. S. Phelps, R. E. Waggoner, and W. C. Leyshon, 1967. Catawba Indians: Morphology, Genetics, and History. *American Journal of Physical Anthropology* 26:5-14.

Pollitzer, W. S., and W. H. Brown, 1969. Survey of Demography, Anthropometry, and Genetics in the Melungeons of Tennessee: An Isolate of Hybrid Origin in Process of Dissolution. *Human Biology* 41:388-400.

Pollitzer, W. S., D. Rucknagel, R. Tashian, D. C. Shreffler, W. C. Leyshon, K. Namboodiri, and R. C. Elston, 1970. The Seminole Indians of Florida: Morphology and Serology. *American Journal of Physical Anthropology* 32:65-82.

Price, E. T., 1950. Mixed-blood Populations of Eastern United States as to Origins, Localizations, and Persistence. Diss. University of California.

Rife, David C., 1968. Finger and Palmar Dermatoglyphics in Seminole Indians of Florida. *American Journal of Physical Anthropology* 28:119-126.

Shim, B-S., and A. G. Bearn, 1964. The Distribution of Haptoglobin Subtypes in Various Populations, including Subtype Patterns in Some Nonhuman Primates. *American Journal of Human Genetics* 16:477-483.

Schneider, R. G., M. E. Haggard, C. W. McNutt, J. E. Johnson, Jr., B. H. Bowman, and D. R. Barnett, 1964. Hemoglobin $G_{Coushatta}$: A New Variant in an American Indian Family. *Science* 143:697-698.

Sigmon, B.A., 1963. A Preliminary Investigation of the Skeletal Material from six Roanoke River Basin Sites. Unpublished Honor's Thesis, University of North Carolina.

Skårland, Ivar, 1939. The Skeletal Material. In *The Chiggerville Site, Site 1, Ohio County, Kentucky*, W. S. Webb and W. G. Haag, eds. *University of Kentucky Reports in Anthropology and Archeology*, 4 (University of Kentucky Press), pp. 28-49.

Snow, Charles E., 1945. Tchefuncte Skeletal Remains. In *The Tchefuncte Culture, an Early Occupation of the Lower Mississippi Valley,* J. A. Ford and G. I. Quimby, Jr., eds. *Memoirs of the Society of American Archeology.* Supplement to *American Antiquity* Vol. X, No. 3, Part 2.

————————————————— , 1948. Indian Knoll Skeletons of Site Oh 2, Ohio County, Kentucky. *University of Kentucky Reports in Anthropology*, IV, No. 3, Part II (University of Kentucky Press).

St. Hoyme, L. E., and W. M. Bass, 1962. Human Skeletal Remains from the Tolliferro (Ha6) and Clarksville (Mc14) Sites, John H. Kerr Reservoir Basin, Virginia. In *Archeology of the John H. Kerr Reservoir Basin, Roanoke River, Virginia-North Carolina*, Carl F. Miller, ed. Bureau of American Ethnology Bulletin, 182: 329-400 (Washington, D.C.: GPO).

Stewart, T. D., 1941. Skeletal Remains from Peachtree Site, North Carolina. In *The Peachtree Site*, F. M. Setzler, and J. D. Jennings, eds. Bureau of American Ethnology Bulletin, 131 (Washington, D.C.: GPO).

Stewart, T. D., and L. G. Quade, 1969. Lesions of the Frontal Bone in American Indians. *American Journal of Physical Anthropology* 30:89-110.

Swanton, John R., 1946. *The Indians of the Southeastern United States.* Bureau of American Ethnology Bulletin, 137 (Washington, D.C.: GPO).

Von Bonin, G., and G. M. Morant, 1938. Indian Races of the United States. A Survey of Previously Published Cranial Measurements. *Biometrika* 30:94-129.

Webb, W. S., and C. E. Snow, 1945. *The Adena People.* University of Kentucky Reports in Anthropology and Archeology, Vol. VI (University of Kentucky Press).

Southeastern Indian Linguistics

MARY R. HAAS

IT is a commonplace of anthropological literature that the greatest linguistic diversity of aboriginal North America was that found in the California-Oregon area. But we know this largely because the northern part of the area was little affected by the inroads of European civilization until around the middle of the nineteenth century. By that time some travelers and investigators were accustomed to taking down vocabularies and other notes on the various tribes that they encountered and hence considerable information about diversity was rather quickly acquired.

Another area of great linguistic diversity in North America was certainly the Southeast and the adjacent coast of the Gulf of Mexico. However, it is seldom spoken of in these terms and is certainly not likely to be compared to California. The principal reason for this is the far greater period of contact—nearly five centuries—and the sparseness of information about the most critical period, namely that before the tribes had been seriously dislocated by the pressures of the competing European nations.

Many smaller tribes in the Southeast have almost certainly vanished without a trace. Others are known to us by name only, and in this event (in spite of frequent claims to the contrary) linguistic affiliation is unknown. Our knowledge of Southeastern linguistics, then, is based on information about some of the larger and more powerful tribes of the area, such as the Cherokee, the Creek, and the Choctaw, and only rarely on the much smaller ones, such as the Biloxi, the Ofo, or the Tunica.

Near the turn of the nineteenth century, spurred by the publication of Pallas's *Vocabularia Comparativa*, a great deal of attention among scholars was turned to the problem of classifying North American languages. The determination of "how many principal stocks, or families there are in North America" (Pickering 1831:581)

was a pressing problem. In 1787 Jefferson (1964:97) had surmised
that their number would be very great. Pickering, unfortunately
swayed in part by theological considerations, believed they would
be "very few in number." Following Duponceau, he surmised that
there were only "three, or at most, four principal stocks" east of
the Mississippi (including the Northeast). Most of the Southeast
was lumped into one stock, the "Floridian" or "Southern" (Pickering
1833). Although Barton (1797:lxvii-lxviii) had correctly postulated
the affiliation between Cherokee and the languages of the "Six
Nations" and also that between Muskogee or Creek and Choctaw-
Chickasaw as early as 1797, his correct guesses were lost in a
maze of incorrect ones and therefore the opportunity to begin
a proper evaluation of the Southeastern situation was lost (Haas
1970). Duponceau's Floridian stock ignored Barton's surmises and
lumped Cherokee in with Creek and Choctaw and other southern
languages.

The first reasonably comprehensive vocabulary of the indigenous
languages north of Mexico was that compiled by Gallatin (1836).
At that time he believed that he had been able to ascertain the
languages of all tribes east of the Mississippi except one. This
was the Alabama-Koasati which, though known to be a part of
the Creek Confederacy, was not known to have had its language
recorded. Gallatin believed that Creek and Choctaw-Chickasaw were
related but he kept them separate until 1848, and, still lacking
vocabularies of Alabama and Koasati, he left them unclassified.

Gallatin's 1836 classification of the languages of the Southeast
was the most accurate that had been achieved to that time. He
dispensed with Duponceau's "Floridean" and strictly separated all
languages whose affinity was in the slightest doubt. This gave
him the following scheme: Atakapa, Chitimacha, Cherokee (possibly
related to Iroquois), Choctaw (possibly related to Muskogee), Catawba (and Woccon), Muskogee (Muskogee proper [Creek], Hitchiti,
and Seminole; possibly related to Choctaw), Natchez, Tunica, Yuchi,
and Timucua. It is interesting that at this time no Siouan tribe
was known to live east of the Mississippi, since Biloxi and Tutelo
had not yet been identified, and Ofo was not known still to exist.
Catawba, though known, was too divergent to be recognized as
being related to the known Siouan languages west of the Mississippi.
It is also important to remember that Gallatin sagaciously classified
only languages for which he had vocabularies, and by 1836 an
unknown number of Southeastern languages had already disappeared.

By the time Powell published his comprehensive scheme for

North America north of Mexico (1891), several problems had
been cleared up and his basic results for the Southeast have been
little modified since. Cherokee, thanks to Hale (1883a), was recognized as the southernmost branch of the Iroquoian family; Alabama
and Koasati, thanks to Gatschet (1884), were correctly placed
in the Muskogean family; and Tutelo and Biloxi, thanks to Hale
(1883b) and Dorsey (1893), were correctly identified as Siouan.
Ofo remained unknown except as one of many unclassified Southeastern tribes known by name only.

Within a couple of decades after the publication of Powell's
classification a flurry of reductionism set in. It seems to have started
with Dixon and Kroeber (1913a, b) who, not content to allow
the California languages to be divided up into 22 unrelated families,
sought to establish interrelationships among them. At about the
same time Swanton began trying to find interrelationships among
the language isolates and language families of the Southeast. The
best known language isolates of the Southeast are Tunica, Chitimacha, Atakapa, Natchez, Yuchi, and Timucua. The most widely
accepted suggestions were that Tunica, Chitimacha, and Atakapa
were three branches of a stock named 'Tunican' (Swanton 1919),
that Natchez was a relative of the Muskogean family (Swanton
1924), and that Yuchi was a relative of the Siouan family (Sapir
1921). There was somewhat more uncertainty about Timucua,
though it was suggested that it might be an outlying relative of
Muskogean (Swanton 1929).

The greatest reduction for North America was finally achieved
by Sapir (1929), who divided up all the languages north of Mexico
into six superstocks. The grandest amalgamation of all was the
one called Hokan-Siouan which encompassed not only many California and Texas languages but also all of the various groupings
that had been arrived at for the Southeast. In California, as it
turned out, Sapir's scheme still allowed the appearance of several
different colors on the map (since five of his superstocks were
represented there) but in the Southeast all differentiation was obliterated in the one color assigned to Hokan-Siouan (Voegelin and
Voegelin 1941).

Whatever the final judgment may be about the eventual accuracy
of Sapir's classification, the immediate result was unfortunate for
Southeastern linguistics since it oversimplified the picture. When
this was added to the already complacent attitude toward Southeastern linguistics due to the feeling of familiarity occasioned by
five centuries of white contact, it is scarcely to be wondered that

there was very little interest in studying the languages of this area.

Boas, however, was not inclined to allow himself to be unduly influenced by the classificatory schemes of his famous students, Kroeber and Sapir. It was part of his overall plan that each linguistic family and language isolate should be adequately described, and so it is perhaps to Boas, more than anyone else, we owe the credit for not allowing interest in Southeastern linguistics to die out prematurely. He seems to have been particularly concerned about the language isolates, less about additional languages belonging to already known families. Hence, in the 1920s and 30s he sent out Wagner to do Yuchi, Swadesh to do Chitimacha, and Haas to do Tunica and Natchez. Though much of this material still remains to be published, texts and a grammar of Yuchi have appeared (Wagner 1931; 1933-38), several special studies of Chitimacha are available (Swadesh 1933; 1934; 1946), and a complete grammar, texts, and dictionary of Tunica have been published (Haas 1940a; 1946; 1950b; 1953).

Boas's foresight in regard to these languages was commendable. Atakapa was already gone in the 1930s, though Swadesh and I attempted to find speakers,[1] and today Tunica, Chitimacha, and Natchez are also extinct. Having been exposed to Southeastern linguistics through my work on Tunica and Natchez, I saw that the proposed affiliations of these language isolates could not be validated (or invalidated) without considerably more information about the Muskogean languages, the largest linguistic family existing solely in the Southeast, and so I also worked extensively on Creek (Haas 1938; 1940; 1948), to a lesser extent on Koasati (Haas 1944), and briefly on Hitchiti and Choctaw.

II

World War II was an exceedingly disruptive influence in the study of North American Indian languages. Almost all the linguists who had had field experience with these languages were diverted to the study and teaching of languages of the Far East considered critical for the war effort and some of them were more or less permanently diverted from their earlier interests. Southeastern Indian linguistics was particularly hard hit. After the work of the 1930s little additional field work was undertaken until fairly recently. Frank T. Siebert followed up the work of Frank Speck on Catawba and presented morphological evidence for the Siouan affinity of the language (Siebert 1945). Ernest Bender (1948), Bender and Zellig Harris (1946), and W. D. Reyburn (1953, 1954) have written on the phonology and verb morphology of Cherokee. Hans Wolff collected and published some additional Yuchi materials (1948). David West is working among the Mikasuki and has published on the phonology (1962). Earl Rand has made a brief study of Alabama and published a phonemic treatment (1968). Still more recently T. Dale Nicklas has undertaken fresh field work on Choctaw, a language which has received very little attention since Byington (1915).

In recent years there have also been some changes in our thinking about linguistic classification problems. It was natural that this work should begin with a rechecking of some of the proposals made by Swanton, particularly in regard to Tunican (Tunica-Chitimacha-Ata- kapa) and to Natchez-Muskogean. Swadesh made a sophisticated study of a part of the first of these in his "Phonologic Formulas for Atakapa- Chitimacha" (1946). Not long after this I proposed putting both of Swanton's groupings into one larger one called "Gulf" (Haas 1951; 1952) and also made note of a few Siouan resemblances. All of this remained ostensibly within the framework of Sapir's Hokan- Siouan superstock. A few years later, however, it became clear that attempts to validate Sapir's far-flung superstock had not been overly successful and that it might be well to look for connections between the Gulf languages and linguistic families outside of Hokan- Siouan. As a result of an effort of this sort it was proposed (Haas 1958) that the Gulf languages might be related to the Algonkian languages (including the Wiyot and Yurok languages of California). Not long after this, following up an earlier suggestion of Louis Allen (1931), Wallace Chafe presented new material supporting the relationship of Siouan and Iroquoian (1964). As a result of these efforts and similar efforts in regard to other parts of North America a considerably modified classification for the continent was set forth in a recent map (Voegelin and Voegelin 1966). The largest of Sapir's six groupings were broken up into smaller groupings, mostly of a more conservative nature. In the Southeast, however, the re- alignment was partly more conservative and partly more radical, as has just been shown.

Linguistic prehistory is often thought of in terms of language classification, as just discussed, but there are other more painstaking kinds of problems to be attacked by the linguistic prehistorian. The most important of these is the reconstruction of protolanguages. The optimum conditions for the reconstruction of a protolanguage require adequate synchronic descriptions of several languages the time depth of whose relation is around 2000 years and the reconstructed result is parts of a language that was spoken around two millennia ago. The only linguistic family lying wholly within the Southeast is Muskogean and here considerable progress has been made in reconstruction (Haas 1941, 1946, 1947, 1949, 1950). Much more remains to be done, however, and for this work fuller descriptive materials on some of the languages are urgently needed, particularly Choctaw-Chickasaw and Alabama.

Several other linguistic families which have branches extending into the Southeast have also seen important progress in the reconstruction of their protolanguages. Foremost among these is Algonkian, for which we have the largest body of reconstructed material of any protolanguage north of Mexico (Bloomfield 1946, Hockett 1957, Siebert 1967). Much progress has also been made in the reconstruction of Proto-Siouan, particularly in the work of Wolff (1950-51) and Matthews (ms. 1958 and 1970). Proto-Iroquoian could also be reconstructed, though Floyd Lounsbury who has presumably worked out quite a lot of it has published almost nothing of it (1961).

The work of reconstructing these protolanguages is a new phase in the progress and development of Southeastern linguistic studies. Nothing of any significance had been done in the reconstruction of any American Indian protolanguage prior to 1925 and most of the work has been done in the past twenty or thirty years. It is here that the pioneering work of Sapir and Bloomfield assumes great significance because it is they and their students (and their students' students) who have made the most important contributions to our knowledge in this area.

The reconstruction of these protolanguages, and the publication of the results, is important not only for Southeastern protolinguistics but for Southeastern protoculture as well, but the development of this possibility in Southeastern studies has not yet been undertaken in any serious way. Some idea of the sorts of things that might be done can be seen in Siebert's careful identification of many flora and fauna which he used in his attempt to determine "The Original Home of the Proto-Algonquian People" (1967).

III

The full extent of linguistic diversity in the Southeast may never be known. Names like Avoyel, Taensas, Koroa, Grigra, Tiou, Yamasee, and Calusa, and many, many others remain to haunt us. Even though some of these have been asserted to be the "same as" or "closely related to" other known languages, we can never be sure in any case where no vocabularies exist. After all, Ofo was thought to be Muskogean because a Tunica Indian recalled one word of the language which began with an /f/ and this was taken to be diagnostic. (Although /f/ is common in Muskogean languages it is rare otherwise.) But when a full vocabulary was finally obtained (Swanton 1909), it was seen to be incontrovertably Siouan. Avoyel and Taensas are said to be related to Natchez on the basis of statements by early missionaries, and Taensas has even been the subject of a grammar generally considered to be a hoax (Brinton 1890:452-67; Swanton 1911:10-13), but whether Avoyel and Taensas were really related to Natchez may never be known. In the same way Koroa, Grigra, and Tiou are said to have been related to Tunica, but again we cannot be sure. But if they were separate languages related to Tunica (and not merely mutually intelligible dialects), their loss is perhaps even greater than if they were totally unrelated, for material on them would have enabled us to reconstruct a Proto-Tunican instead of having to deal with Tunica as a language isolate.

But quite aside from the problem of the unclassified languages of the Southeast, we have good reason to believe that the area was exceeded in diversity only by California-Oregon and the Northwest. If we take a time depth of about two millennia as our base, we find the following families represented in the Southeast, viz:

Algonkian (e. g. Powhatan, Pamlico, and others; Shawnee)

Iroquoian (Tuscarora and Cherokee, and probably some others)

Siouan (e. g. Tutelo, Biloxi, Ofo, and others; more distantly, Catawba)

Muskogean (Choctaw-Chickasaw, Apalachee, Alabama, Koasati, Hitchiti, Mikasuki, Creek, and probably others).

Besides these families we have several language isolates in the area, some of which may be related to one of the above families at a time depth in excess of two millennia, viz:

Yuchi (probably related to Proto-Siouan)

Natchez (related to Proto-Muskogean)

Tunica (part of Gulf, including Chitimacha, Atakapa, Natchez, and Proto-Muskogean)

Chitimacha (part of Gulf, as above)

Atakapa (part of Gulf, as above)

Timucua (of doubtful affiliation, Muskogean? Siouan? Arawakan?)[2]

The answer to the question of what these languages reflect of conditions of four or more millennia ago is suggested by various proposals of wider connections, e. g., Algonkian-Gulf, Siouan-Iroquoian, and even Sapir's Hokan-Siouan. Moreover, even though little has been done in the way of comparisons of North and South American languages, the possibility of finding connections should be good in the Southeast because of its proximity to the Caribbean area. However, greater certainty in regard to any proposals of more distant connections must await a greater accumulation of actual reconstructions in the strategic protolanguages of both continents, a task which may require decades. But this work, as it progresses, will be important for all kinds of prehistorical knowledge of the area, including possible South American connections. Southeastern Indian linguistics is clearly not a thing of the past but an endeavor which is only seriously beginning and which has a very bright future indeed.

NOTES

1. We also attempted to find speakers of other dying languages of the Southeast but succeeded only in the case of Biloxi for which a vocabulary of 54 words was collected (Haas 1968).

2. A possible Muskogean affiliation was suggested by Swanton in 1929. More recently Swadesh (1964) noted a small number of Arawakan resemblances but Siouan resemblances of a similar nature can also be found.

REFERENCES

Allen, Louis, 1931. Siouan and Iroquoian. *International Journal of American Linguistics* 6:185-193.
Barton, Benjamin Smith, 1797. *New Views of the Origin of the Tribes and Nations of North America* (Philadelphia: John Bioren).
Bender, Ernest, 1949. Cherokee II. *International Journal of American Linguistics* 15:223-228.
─────────── and Zellig S. Harris, 1946. The Phonemes of North Carolina Cherokee. *International Journal of American Linguistics* 12:14-21.
Bloomfield, Leonard, 1946. Algonquian. In *Linguistic Structures of Native America*, Harry Hoijer et al., Viking Fund Publications in Anthropology, no. 6, pp. 85-129.
Brinton, Daniel G., 1890. The Curious Hoax of the Taensa Language. *Essays of an Americanist* (Philadelphia: David McKay), pp. 452-467.
Byington, Cyrus A., 1915. *A Dictionary of the Choctaw Language*. Bureau of American Ethnology Bulletin 46 (Washington, D.C.: GPO).
Chafe, Wallace L., 1964. Another Look at Siouan and Iroquoian. *American Anthropologist* 66:852-862.
Dixon, Roland B. and Alfred L. Kroeber, 1913a. Relationship of the Indian Languages of California. *Science*, n.s., 37:225.
───────────, 1913b. New Linguistic Families in California. *American Anthropologist*, n.s., 15:647-655.
Dorsey, James Owen, 1893. *The Biloxi Indians of Louisiana*. American Association for the Advancement of Science Proceedings 43:267-287.

Gallatin, Albert, 1836. *A Synopsis of the Indian Tribes within the United States*. . . . Transactions and Collections of the American Antiquarian Society, 2:1-422.

—————————————————, 1848. *Hale's Indians of North-West America, and Vocabularies of North America*. . . . Transactions of the American Ethnological Society, 2:xxiii-clxxx, 1-130.

Gatschet, Albert S., 1884. *A Migration Legend of the Creek Indians*, Brinton's Library of Aboriginal American Literature, I, no. 4. (Philadelphia).

Haas, Mary R., 1938. Geminate Consonant Clusters in Muskogee. *Language* 14:61-65.

—————————————————, 1940a. Tunica. Extract from *Handbook of American Indian Languages*, Part 4, Franz Boas, ed. (New York: Augustin).

—————————————————, 1940b. Ablaut and its Function in Muskogee. *Language* 16:141-150.

—————————————————, 1941. The Classification of the Muskogean Languages. In *Language, Culture, and Personality*, Leslie Spier, A. Irving Hallowell, and Stanley S. Newman, eds. (Menasha, Wisconsin).

—————————————————, 1944. Men's and Women's Speech in Koasati. *Language* 20:142-149

—————————————————, 1946a. A Grammatical Sketch of Tunica. In *Linguistic Structures of Native America*, Harry Hoijer et al., Viking Fund Publications in Anthropology, no. 6, pp. 337-366.

—————————————————, 1946b. A Proto-Muskogean Paradigm. *Language* 22:326-332.

—————————————————, 1947. Development of Proto-Muskogean *k^w. *International Journal of American Linguistics* 13:135-137.

—————————————————, 1948. Classificatory Verbs in Muskogee. *International Journal of American Linguistics* 14:244-246.

—————————————————, 1949. The Position of Apalachee in the Muskogean Family. *International Journal of American Linguistics* 15:121-127.

—————————————————, 1950a. The Historical Development of Certain Long Vowels in Creek. *International Journal of American Linguistics* 16:122-125.

—————————————————, 1950b. *Tunica Texts*, University of California Publications in Linguistics 6:1-174 (Berkeley and Los Angeles).

—————————————————, 1951. The Proto-Gulf Word for *Water* (with Notes on Siouan-Yuchi). *International Journal of American Linguistics* 17:71-79.

—————————————————, 1952. The Proto-Gulf Word for *Land* (with a note on Proto-Siouan). *International Journal of American Linguistics* 18:238-240.

—————————————————, 1953. *Tunica Dictionary*, University of California Publications in Linguistics 6:175-332 (Berkeley and Los Angeles).

—————————————————, 1956. Natchez and the Muskogean Languages. *Language* 32:61-72.

—————————————————, 1958. A New Linguistic Relationship in North America: Algonkian and the Gulf Languages. *Southwestern Journal of Anthropology* 14:231-264.

—————————————————, 1968. The Last Words of Biloxi. *International Journal of American Linguistics* 34:77-84.

—————————————————, 1969. *The Prehistory of Languages*, Janua Linguarum, series minor, no. 57 (The Hague-Paris: Mouton).

—————————————————, 1970. Review of Benjamin Smith Barton, New Views of the Origin of the Tribes and Nations of North America. (Ann Arbor, Michigan: University Microfilms, 1968). *International Journal of American Linguistics* 36:68-70.

Hale, Horatio, 1883a. Indian Migrations, as Evidenced by Language, Part I: The Huron-Cherokee Stock. *The American Antiquarian* 5:18-28.

--------------------------------, 1883*b*. The Tutelo Tribe and Language. *Proceedings of the American Philosophical Society* 21:1-45 (Philadelphia).

Hockett, Charles F., 1957. Central Algonquian Vocabulary: Stems in /k-/. *International Journal of American Linguistics* 23:247-268.

Jefferson, Thomas, 1964. *Notes on the State of Virginia.* Harper Torchbooks TB 3052 (New York, Evanston, London: Harper and Row).

Lounsbury, Floyd G., 1961. Iroquois-Cherokee Linguistic Relations. *Symposium on Cherokee-Iroquois Culture.* Bureau of American Ethnology Bulletin 180 (Washington, D.C.: GPO).

Matthews, G. Hubert, [1958]. Handbook of Siouan Languages. University of Pennsylvania dissertation.

--------------------------------, 1959. Proto-Siouan Kinship Terminology. *American Anthropologist* 61:252-278.

--------------------------------, 1970. Some Notes on the Proto-Siouan Continuants. *International Journal of American Linguistics* 35:98-109.

[Pickering, John], 1831. Indian Languages of America. *Encyclopaedia Americana* Vol. IV (Appendix), pp. 581-900.

--------------------------------; 1833. Introductory Memoir. Father Sebastian Rasles, A Dictionary of the Abnaki Language, American Academy of Arts and Sciences Memoir 1:370-574, pp. 371-372.

Powell, John Wesley, 1891. *Linguistic Families of North America North of Mexico.* Seventh Annual Report, Bureau of [American] Ethnology, 1885-1886, pp. 1-142.

Rand, Earl, 1968. The Structural Phonology of Alabaman, a Muskogean Language. *International Journal of American Linguistics* 34:94-103.

Reyburn, William D., 1953. Cherokee Verb Morphology I. *International Journal of American Linguistics* 19:172-180.

Sapir, Edward, 1920. The Hokan and Coahuiltecan Languages. *International Journal of American Linguistics* 1:280-290.

--------------------------------, 1921. A Bird's-eye View of American Languages North of Mexico. *Science* 54:408.

--------------------------------, 1929. Central and North American Indian Languages. *The Encyclopaedia Britannica,* 14th ed., 5:138-141 (London, New York, and Toronto: The Encyclopaedia Britannica Co.). Reprinted in *Selected Writings of Edward Sapir,* David G. Mandelbaum, ed. (Berkeley and Los Angeles: The University of California Press, 1949).

Siebert, Frank T., Jr., 1945. Linguistic Classification of Catawba. *International Journal of American Linguistics* 11:100-104, 211-218.

--------------------------------, 1967. The Original Home of the Proto-Algonquian People. National Museum of Canada Bulletin, 214: Contributions to Anthropology: Linguistics I, pp. 13-47 (Ottawa: The Queen's Printer).

Swadesh, Morris, 1933. Chitimacha Verbs of Derogatory or Abusive Connotation. *Language* 9:192-201.

--------------------------------, 1934. The Phonetics of Chitimacha. *Language* 10:345-362.

--------------------------------, 1946*a*. Chitimacha. In *Linguistic Structures of Native America,* Harry Hoijer et al., Viking Fund Publications in Anthropology, no. 6, pp. 312-336.

--------------------------------, 1946*b*. Phonologic formulas for Atakapa-Chitimacha. *International Journal of American Linguistics* 12:113-132.

--------------------------------, 1947. Atakapa-Chitimacha *k^w*. *International Journal of American Linguistics* 13:120-121.

--------------------------------, 1964. Linguistic Overview. In *Prehistoric Man in the New World,* Jesse D. Jennings and Edward Norbeck, eds. (Chicago: The University of Chicago Press), pp. 527-556.

Swanton, John R., 1909. A New Siouan Dialect. *Putnam Anniversary Volume* (New York), pp. 477-486.

——————————————, 1911. *Indian Tribes of the Lower Mississippi Valley and Adjacent Coast of the Gulf of Mexico.* Bureau of American Ethnology Bulletin 43 (Washington: GPO).

——————————————, 1919. A Structural and Lexical Comparison of the Tunica, Chitimacha, and Atakapa Languages. Bureau of American Ethnology Bulletin 68 (Washington: GPO).

——————————————, 1924. The Muskhogean Connection of the Natchez Language. *International Journal of American Linguistics* 3:46-75.

——————————————, 1929. The Tawasa Language. *American Anthropologist* 31:435-453.

——————————————, 1946. *The Indians of the Southeastern United States.* Bureau of American Ethnology Bulletin 137 (Washington: GPO).

Voegelin, Charles F. and Erminie Wheeler Voegelin, 1941. Map of North American Indian Languages (Menasha, Wisconsin: American Ethnological Society).

Voegelin, Charles F. and Florence M. Voegelin, 1966. Map of North American Indian Languages (Rand, McNally, and Co.: American Ethnological Society).

Wagner, Günter, 1931. *Yuchi Tales.* Publications of the American Ethnological Society, vol. 13.

——————————————, 1933-38. Yuchi. In *Handbook of American Indian Languages,* Part 3, Franz Boas, ed. (Glückstadt-Hamburg-New York: Augustin).

West, John David, 1962. The Phonology of Mikasuki. *Studies in Linguistics* 16:77-91.

Wolff, Hans, 1948. Yuchi Phonemes and Morphemes, with Special Reference to Person Markers. *International Journal of American Linguistics* 14:240-243.

——————————————, 1950-51. Comparative Siouan I, II, III, IV. *International Journal of American Linguistics* 26:61-66, 113-121, 168-178; 27:197-204.

——————————————, 1951. Yuchi Text with Analysis. *International Journal of American Linguistics* 17:48-53.

The Archaeology of European-Indian Contact in the Southeast

David J. Hally

This paper is intended as a review and critique of historic archaeology in the Southeastern United States. For our purposes here, historic archaeology may be defined, following Fontana (1965:61), as "archaeology carried out in sites which contain material evidence of non-Indian culture or concerning which there is contemporary non-Indian documentary record." In the Southeast, this definition encompasses a period of nearly five centuries, but in the present paper we will be concerned with only the 350 years of European-Indian contact preceding Indian removal in 1838. Our geographical focus will be that area which the historian Verner W. Crane calls the Southern Frontier—"the great area extending southward from Virginia and the Tennessee Valley to the Gulf of Mexico, and westward to the Mississippi River" (Crane 1956:v).

In the Southeast to date, approximately one hundred and forty historic sites have been investigated and described in print.[1] Of these, the great majority, roughly 75%, are aboriginal sites yielding evidence of European contact. The remainder are the direct result of European activity; they include missions, forts, trading posts, habitations, and miscellaneous sites such as fishing camps and ship wrecks of the Spanish Plate fleet.

A number of aboriginal sites can be identified with reasonable certainty in the historical records of the 16th through 19th centuries. A complete inventory of these is not possible here, but some idea of the geographical and cultural range they represent can be given in a selected listing. In the lower Mississippi Valley, several sites can be identified: the Fatherland site, the Grand Village of the Natchez from 1682 to 1729 (Neitzel 1965); the Haynes Bluff and Angola Farm sites, representing historic Tunica from 1698 to approximately 1800 (Ford 1936:101-2, 129-40); and the Bayou Goula

site, with a checkered occupational history spanning the years 1699
to 1758 and including remnants of the Bayogoula, Mugulasha, Aco-
lapissa, Tiou, Taensa, Chitimacha, and Houma (Quimby 1957).
Documented Cherokee sites are represented by the lower settlement
of Chauga (Kelly and Neitzel 1961), the eighteenth century Overhill
towns of Chote and Ocoee (Lewis 1953), and New Echota, the
capital of the Cherokee Nation from 1826 to 1830 (DeBaillou 1955).
In Georgia, the eighteenth century Lower Creek town of Kasita
(Willey and Sears 1952) and Palachacolas, an Apalachicola settlement on the Savannah River dating to 1684-1716 (J. Caldwell 1948),
have been identified and reported on briefly. Documented, aboriginal
sites in Florida include Safety Harbor, principal town of the Toco-
bago visited by Governor Menendez in 1567 (Griffin and Bullen
1950) and Mound Key, the Calusa capital visited by Menendez in
the following year (Goggin and Sturtevant 1964).

In some cases, sites that are not specifically documented can
nevertheless be attributed with reasonable certainty to historically
known tribal or ethnic groups. The four sites excavated by Jennings
(1941) near Tupelo, Mississippi, and identified as Chickasaw are
good examples of this kind of situation.

With these two kinds of identification, it is possible to define
the archaeological culture of several tribal groups for at least one
point in their historically documented existence. These include Natchez (Neitzel 1965), Taensa (Williams 1967), Tunica (Ford 1936),
Coosa (DeJarnette and Hansen 1960), Kasita (Willey and Sears 1952),
Apalachicola (Caldwell 1948), Hitchiti (Kelly 1938; Fairbanks 1956),
Yuchi (Chase 1960), Tocobaga (Griffin and Bullen 1950), Potano
(Goggin et al. 1949), Calusa (Goggin and Sturtevant 1964), and at least
one segment of the Chickasaw (Jennings 1941), Choctaw (Collins
1927), Overhill Cherokee (Lewis 1953), Underhill Cherokee (Kelly
and Neitzel 1961), Guale (Larson 1958), and Seminole (Goggin
1949; Bullen 1953). These identifications are, theoretically at least,
datum points from which further investigations concerned with
tribal histories or acculturation processes can be undertaken.

European sites that have been identified and investigated include,
among others, the Castillo de San Marcos (Harrington et al. 1955),
Fort Frederica (Manucy 1962), the Spanish missions of San Francisco
de Oconee and San Luis (Boyd et al. 1951), Charles Towne (Stephenson 1969), and an English trading post, Spaulding's Lower Store,
serving the Seminole from 1763 to 1784 (Goggin 1949).

In the past several years, an increasing effort has been devoted
to the analysis of European artifacts found on historic sites. Recent

typological and documentary studies have provided information on developmental changes that specific kinds of artifacts have undergone and on the manufacturing and trade systems that brought them to the New World. Outstanding studies include those of John M. Goggin on Spanish pottery of the olive jar (1960) and majolica (1968) types, John Witthoft on gun flints (1966), and Stanley J. Olsen on plain clothing buttons of the 18th and 19th centuries (1963). The most immediate reward of this kind of research is an increased precision in historic site chronology. In addition, knowledge of the European origin of trade materials may assist in identifying the nationality of non-aboriginal sites, as well as provide insight into trade patterns within the Southeast. Of potentially great value in this regard is Witthoft's (1966:24-5) recent observation that Spanish gun flints are derived from Albanian quarries and are distinguishable from North European flints used by French and English.

The archaeological literature yields a number of insights into the effect of European contact on aboriginal Southeastern culture. Several researchers have noted the persistence of aboriginal pottery making well into the historic period. At the Upper Creek towns of Nuyake and Tohopeka, both destroyed during the Creek war of 1813-1814, Fairbanks (1962:42, 51) found pottery very similar to that of the related Ocmulgee Fields culture which is dated at approximately 1685-1715. One hundred years of intensive contact with whites seems to have had little effect on the ceramic arts of these people. Fairbanks (1962:51-3) and Mason (1963:73) both attribute this conservatism to the nature of European contact, which affected women's roles little, and to the stabilizing nature of the matrilineal organization of Creek society.

Among the mission Indians of Guale, Apalachee, and Timucua provinces, pottery making continued apparently until the complete destruction of the mission system by English-Indian raids between 1700 and 1725. Unlike the English, the Spanish traditionally used earthenware vessels in food preparation. Majolica and olive jars, the only Spanish pottery occurring with any regularity and frequency in Florida sites, were apparently used for food storage and consumption. Indian pottery seems to have been used for cooking (Goggin 1952:72; Smith 1956:105), and it is likely that the Spanish actually encouraged this aboriginal craft.

Perhaps the contact situation with greatest potential for Indian acculturation prevailed in the Spanish mission system of north Florida. Available archaeological evidence, however, indicates that the missions had relatively little effect on native culture. As noted, aboriginal pottery making continued throughout the mission period. Much of the aboriginal tool inventory seems also to have been retained. Among the artifacts recovered during the excavation of the Apalachee mission of San Francisco de Oconee are stone projectile points, scrapers, and mauls, limestone awl sharpeners, and grinding stones (Boyd et al. 1950:175-7).

The effectiveness of the Spanish policy of Christianizing the native population is difficult to assess archaeologically. A measure of success is perhaps indicated by the cessation of burial mound construction in the Apalachee and Timucua territories by 1600 (Smith 1956:37). To the south, beyond direct Spanish control, this aboriginal mortuary practice persisted well into the 17th century (Smith 1956:64). On the other hand, lack of success can be inferred from the fact that no examples of native made religious articles showing Christian influence have been reported from any site in Spanish Florida.

The extent to which the mission system affected native settlement patterns is uncertain. There were apparently efforts to consolidate the native population in mission settlements, but these seem to have been largely unsuccessful due to the requirements of Indian subsistence practices (Sturtevant 1962:57, 62). Archaeological evidence bearing on this question is inconclusive. At Darien Bluff site (S. Caldwell 1954:15-16), possibly the mission of Santo Domingo de Talaje, we find evidence of a nucleated settlement consisting of fifteen wall trench structures "neatly arranged" in an area to the east of buildings identified as the actual mission complex. The Scott Miller site (the mission of San Francisco de Oconee), on the other hand, did not yield evidence of habitation structures for the Indian neophytes despite extensive testing (Boyd et al. 1950:11-24). Evidence of them may have been obliterated by recent plowing, but it is also possible that this mission was characterized by a dispersed settlement pattern.

Aboriginal culture was not alone in undergoing change as a result of European-Indian contact. There is some archaeological evidence that the Spanish way of life was also being modified. Most striking is evidence from the Spanish frontier outpost, Fort Pupo, on the St. Johns River, which shows the extent to which Spaniards in some situations were utilizing aboriginal material culture (Goggin 1951). So small in quantity and variety were the Spanish artifacts at this fort and so abundant those of an aboriginal nature, that the investigator, John Goggin, is led to observe, "If we had no historical evidence for the nature of the inhabitants at Pupo in Spanish times, the most reasonable assumption would be that the site was one purely of Indian occupation" (1951:186).

From historical records, it is clear that there was considerable movement of tribal populations within the Southeast during the contact period. Some documented movements can be recognized archaeologically. Retreat of the aboriginal population from the Georgia coast province of Guale to the vicinity of St. Augustine in the late 17th century is reflected archaeologically in the appearance of San Marcos series pottery in the latter area (Goggin 1952:60-61; Larson 1958:14). It is also possible to archaeologically demonstrate the later arrival in Florida of peoples that came to be known as Seminole (Goggin 1949, 1958). The movement of remnant Natchez groups subsequent to dispersal by French forces in 1730 is documented in the historical records (Swanton 1911: 253-6) and substantiated archaeologically. In two of the four historic Chickasaw sites he investigated near Tupelo, Mississippi, Jennings (1941: 179-80) found abundant sherds of the Natchez pottery types, Fatherland Incised and Natchez Incised.

From the preceding review, it is clear that much has been accomplished in the field of Southeastern historic archaeology. This pleasing picture must be tempered, however, by a consideration of the shortcomings and inadequacies of the field. These, it should be noted, are by no means unique to the Southeast or to the historic period, but rather are characteristic of American archaeology in general. The research under consideration here may be criticized at three points: inadequacy of investigation, inadequacy of reporting, and inadequacy of interpretation.

The simple fact concerning research conducted to date is that roughly 75% of the sites reported have only been investigated by surface artifact collecting, test pit excavation, or amateur excavation. For an additional 10% of the sites, investigation has been concerned only with burials or mounds. As a result, data available for study from an overwhelming majority of the reported sites is limited in kind and is not representative of total cultures. Much of the value of Goggin's research on Fort Pupo (Goggin 1951), for example, lies in his interpretation of the different degree to which the English and Spanish garrisons were affected by Indian culture. This interpretation, however, is based on only two small test trenches, one of which apparently was located beyond the perimeter of the Spanish fortifications. Adequate sampling of the site might have yielded an entirely different picture of the Spanish occupation than is reported.

In my judgment, only eleven historic sites in the entire Southeast have received an adequate amount and kind of investigation. These are Mle 14 and Mle 90 (Jennings 1941), Bayou Goula (Quimby 1957), Chote (Lewis 1953), Macon Trading Post (Kelly 1938), Scott Miller (Boyd et al. 1950), Darien Bluff (S. Caldwell 1954), Charles Towne (Stephenson 1969), Kasita (Willey and Sears 1952), Fort Frederica (Manucy 1962), and Santa Rosa Pensacola (Smith 1965). Unfortunately, several of these sites have been inadequately reported. At the very least, a site report should contain a detailed description of both the artifacts and architectural features encountered and their assignment to components present at the site. Only a small number of historic sites with any kind of professional field investigation have received such treatment in print.

In the majority of published site reports, interpretation is restricted to identifying the site in historical records and determining the cultural affiliation of its occupants. To some extent these limited goals result from the nature of site investigation. Without extensive excavation of some sort, it is difficult to carry interpretation any further. The relationship between field investigation and interpretation, however, is a reciprocal one. If one is interested only in identifying the cultural affiliation of a site, surface collecting and test pits may be completely adequate.

Site reports containing additional interpretation are worth noting if for no other reason than to give their authors the recognition they deserve. Morrell (1965), Jennings (1941), Goggin (1951), and Fairbanks (1962) have each made observations on the consequences of Indian-European contact based upon field data from a particular site. In a number of reports, historical data is utilized as an aid in interpreting the archaeological record. Outstanding in this regard are the analyses of Neitzel (1965) at Fatherland, Quimby (1957) at Bayou Goula, and Manucy (1962) at Fort Frederica. In the latter, we find archaeology and history working together to provide a detailed description of the fort as it once existed.

Without doubt, the finest comparative synthesis available is that of Hale Smith (1956) dealing with the historic period in Florida. In this study, Smith reviews information available on all known historic sites in the state within a chronological framework of three periods spanning the years 1500 to 1800. Archaeological and historical information is presented to indicate the nature and effect of European-Indian contact during these different periods and a comparison is made between the Spanish-Indian and the English-Indian contact situations.

With this one exception, attempts to synthesize all or part of the historic period in the Southeast are concerned primarily with identifying archaeological cultures with tribal or ethnic groups described in historical accounts.[2] This is certainly an important undertaking, but unfortunately the conclusions offered in such studies are of doubtful validity. For one thing, these syntheses suffer as a result of their reliance on three highly questionable assumptions: that material culture, especially pottery, correlates with ethnic, tribal, political, or linguistic boundaries; that change in the archaeological record is due in the main to movements of people; and that the size, composition, and nature of tribal groups recorded by Europeans were invariant from the late prehistoric period through Indian removal. These syntheses are also defective in that they are concerned almost entirely with political and linguistic groupings such as Creek, Upper and Lower Creek, Muskogean, and Timucuan.

The archaeological literature is full of across-the-board identifications of archaeologically defined cultures and historically documented tribal groups. Frequently, we find the archaeologist paying token homage to the anthropological tenet that there is no necessary relationship between pottery or material culture on the one hand and people on the other, and then proceeding to make just such an identification. In one recently published paper (Bullen 1969:417), the Safety Harbor ceramic complex is equated with Timucua, a language family of uncertain linguistic affiliation, and the Glades pottery complex is equated with Calusa, a political entity. A number of articles (Fairbanks 1958; Sears 1955; Kneberg 1952) have appeared concerning the ceramic complexes characteristic of Creek and Cherokee.

The existence of Creek legends indicating a western origin for Muskogean-speaking tribes and the evident intrusion of Mississippian type culture into the Southeast from that general direction in prehistoric times together encourage the assumption that migration has been a major mechanism bringing about culture change. The archaeological cultures Macon Plateau, Dallas, Fort Walton, Pensacola, and Moundville are frequently cited as evidence for the late prehistoric arrival of Muskogean speakers in the Southeast. In eastern Tennessee, one interpretation (Lewis 1943; Kneberg 1952) equates Creek and Yuchi with Mississippian cultures and Cherokee with cultures related to Caldwell's (1958) Southern Appalachian tradition. Logically, the observed archaeological shift from Mississippian to Southern Appalachian culture type in historic times is attributed to the replacement of Creek and Yuchi by Cherokee (Kneberg 1952:197-98).[3]

The assumption that aboriginal tribal units recognized by Europeans were invariant through time is most thoroughly embraced by researchers working with "Creek" prehistory.[4] Categories such as Creek, Upper Creek, and Lower Creek may have had cultural significance in the 18th century, but there is no guarantee, and in fact it is unlikely, that such was the case one hundred or two hundred years earlier. The Creek Confederacy was a political entity made possible in large part by the degree of cultural homogeneity existing throughout the Southeast in aboriginal times. It represented the last large scale political alignment in the area, but descriptions of de Soto's travels indicate it was not the first. To use these terms and categories uncritically in our research and to assume that they necessarily correlate with archaeological cultures of the prehistoric period can only lead to confusion when we attempt to reconstruct culture history.

I do not think we can make much progress in correlating archaeological and ethnohistorical data in the Southeast as long as we continue to concern ourselves with linguistic categories such as Hitchiti and Muskogee or large scale political alignments such as Creek and Apalachee. Rather, we should focus our attention on the individual tribes or towns that comprise these larger entities.[5] Field research should be concentrated on historically identifiable sites of known ethnic composition with the aim of defining the archaeological culture of such towns. Once they have been identified and defined archaeologically, towns such as Kasita and Ocmulgee or Chote and Chauga can then be compared to determine what, if any, archaeological significance the larger tribal groupings such as Creek and Cherokee have.[6]

At the present time, despite the great amount of work that has been done in Southeastern historic archaeology, the field seems to lack direction. I would suggest that there are at least three tasks which are appropriate and reasonable for it: application of the direct historical approach to specific ethnic groups, investigation of European-Indian acculturation, and investigation of the relationship between archaeological culture units and social or ethnic groups. All three goals complement one another. Furthermore, progress in all would seem to require that we concentrate field research upon the remains of historically documented towns.

Ethnohistorical data indicate the persistence of individual towns as distinct entities throughout much of the contact period, Coosa being a good example. It is logical that they be the subject of the direct historical approach rather than entities such as Creek and Cherokee. If Ocmulgee and Kasita or Tocobaga and Potano are archaeologically distinct on the historic horizon, then culture historical reconstruction should begin with them and work backward in time.

If we are to ever have more than general insights into the nature of European-Indian acculturation in the Southeast, it will be necessary to investigate changes through time in specific ethnic groups. What is necessary is to work with the sequentially related settlements of specific towns. We must, for example, have information on the nature and progress of acculturation among the Kashita not only for 1715, but also for 1680 and 1780.

The relationship of the archaeologist's unit concepts—phase, focus, culture, horizon—to ethnic and social groups has received relatively little attention in American archaeology.[7] Yet if we are ever to do more than construct ceramic histories, we must face this question and attempt to discover what, if any, invariant relationships there are. Obviously, the historic period provides us with the most advantageous conditions for tackling the problem. Only in this period is it possible to compare ethnographically defined ethnic groups with archaeologically defined units.

NOTES

1. For practical reasons, it has been necessary to limit the scope of this paper to published research.
2. Cf. Fairbanks (1952), Lewis (1943), Kneberg (1952), and Sears (1955; 1964).
3. This view of Cherokee history has been recently criticized by Joffre Coe (1961).
4. Cf. Fairbanks (1952:294).
5. I have in mind here the towns or *Talwa* of the Creek confederacy which Swanton (1928:242) describes as consisting of a "body of people who had their own square ground and actually formed a little state." Comparable ethnic units existed among the Cherokee. Gearing (1962:3) refers to them as villages and estimates that they numbered between 30 and 40 in the early 18th century.
6. Bruce G. Trigger (1968:20-23) advocates a similar approach for archaeological reconstruction in general when he recommends that we first identify communities—"the archaeologist's socially defined minimal unit"—and then proceed to investigate the cultural, political, economic, and social relationships existing between them.
7. But see Trigger (1968; Chapter 3).

REFERENCES

Boyd, Mark F., Hale G. Smith, and John W. Griffin, 1951. *Here They Once Stood: The Tragic End of the Apalachee Missions* (Gainesville: University of Florida Press).

Bullen, Ripley P., 1953. Notes on the Seminole Archaeology of West Florida. *Southeastern Archaeological Conference Newsletter*, Vol. 3, No. 1.
———————————————, 1969. The Southern Limit of Timucua Territory. *Florida Historical Quarterly* 47:414-419.
Caldwell, Joseph R., 1948. Palachacolas Town, Hampton County, South Carolina. *Journal of the Washington Academy of Science* 38: 321-4.
———————————————, 1958. *Trend and Tradition in the Prehistory of the Eastern United States*. American Anthropological Association Memoirs, No. 88.
Caldwell, Sheila K., 1954. A Spanish Mission Site Near Darien. *Early Georgia* 1:13-17.
Chase, David W., 1960. *An Historic Indian Town Site in Russell County, Alabama*, Coweta Memorial Association Papers, No. 2 (Columbus, Georgia).
Coe, Joffre L., 1961. Cherokee Archaeology. In *Symposium on Cherokee and Iroquois Culture*, William N. Fenton and John Gulick, eds., Bureau of American Ethnology Bulletin, No. 180 (Washington, D.C.: GPO).
Collins, Henry B., 1927. Potsherds from Choctaw Village Sites in Mississippi. *Journal of the Washington Academy of Science* 17: 259-61.
Crane, Verner W., 1956. *The Southern Frontier: 1670-1732* (Ann Arbor: University of Michigan Press).
DeBaillou, Clemens, 1955. Excavations at New Echota in 1954. *Early Georgia*, Vol. 1, No. 4.
DeJarnette, David L. and Asael T. Hansen, 1960. *The Archaeology of the Childersburg Site, Alabama*, Department of Anthropology, Florida State University, Notes in Anthropology, No. 4 (Tallahassee).
Fairbanks, Charles H., 1952. Creek and Pre-Creek. In *Archaeology of Eastern United States*, James B. Griffin, ed. (Chicago: University of Chicago Press), pp. 285-300.
———————————————, 1956. *Archaeology of the Funeral Mound, Ocmulgee National Monument, Georgia*, National Park Service, Archaeological Research Series, No. 3 (Washington, D.C.: GPO).
———————————————, 1958. Some Problems of the Origin of Creek Pottery. *The Florida Anthropologist* 11 (2)53-63.
———————————————, 1962. Excavations at Horseshoe Bend, Alabama. *Florida Anthropologist* 15 (2)41-56.
Fontana, Bernard L., 1965. On the Meaning of Historic Sites Archaeology. *American Antiquity* 31:61-65.
Ford, James A., 1936. *Analysis of Indian Village Site Collections from Louisiana and Mississippi*, Department of Conservation, Louisiana Geological Survey, Anthropological Study, No. 2 (New Orleans).
Gearing, Fred, 1962. *Priests and Warriors: Social Structures for Cherokee Politics in the 18th Century*. American Anthropological Association Memoirs, No. 93.
Goggin, John M., 1949. A Florida Indian Trading Post, Ca. 1673-1784. *Southern Indian Studies*, 1:35-38.
———————————————, 1951. Fort Pupo—A Spanish Frontier Outpost. *Florida Historical Quarterly* 30:139-92.
———————————————, 1952. *Space and Time Perspective in Northern St. Johns Archaeology, Florida*, Yale University Publications in Anthropology, No. 47 (New Haven: Yale University Press).
———————————————, 1958. Seminole Pottery. In *Prehistoric Pottery of the Eastern United States*, Museum of Anthropology, University of Michigan.
———————————————, 1960. *The Spanish Olive Jar*, Yale University Publications in Anthropology, No. 62 (New Haven: Yale University Press).
———————————————, 1968. *Spanish Majolica in the New World: Types of the Sixteenth to Eighteenth Centuries*, Yale University Publication in Anthropology, No. 72 (New Haven: Yale University Press).

Goggin, John M., Mary E. Goodwin, Earl Hester, David Prange, and Robert Spangeberg, 1949. An Historic Indian Burial, Alachua Co., Florida. *Florida Anthropologist* 2:10-25.

Goggin, John M. and William C. Sturtevant, 1964. The Calusa: A Stratified Nonagricultural Society (With Notes on Sibling Marriage). In *Explorations in Cultural Anthropology*, Ward H. Goodenough, ed. (New York: McGraw-Hill), pp. 179-219.

Griffin, John W. and Ripley P. Bullen, 1950. *The Safety Harbor Site, Penellas County, Florida*, Florida Anthropological Society Publications, No. 2 (Gainesville: University of Florida Press).

Griffin, John W. and Hale G. Smith, 1949. Nocoroco, A Timucua Village of 1605 Now in Tomoka State Park. *Florida Historical Quarterly* 27:340-361.

Harrington, J. C., Albert C. Manucy, and John M. Goggin, 1955. Archaeological Excavations in the Courtyard of Castillo de San Marcos, St. Augustine, Florida. *Florida Historical Quarterly* 34:100-141.

Jennings, Jesse D., 1941. Chickasaw and Earlier Indian Cultures of Northeast Mississippi. *Journal of Mississippi History* 3:155-226.

Kelly, A. R., 1938. *A Preliminary Report on Archaeological Explorations at Macon, Georgia*. Bureau of American Ethnology, Bulletin, No. 119 (Washington, D.C.: GPO).

Kelly, A. R. and R. S. Neitzel, 1961. *The Chauga Site in Oconee County, South Carolina*, University of Georgia, Laboratory of Archaeology Series, No. 3 (Athens, Georgia: Department of Sociology and Anthropology).

Kneberg, Madeline, 1952. The Tennessee Area. In *Archaeology of Eastern United States*, James B. Griffin, ed. (Chicago: University of Chicago Press), pp. 190-198.

Larson, Lewis H., 1958. Cultural Relationships Between the Northern St. Johns Area and Georgia Coast. *The Florida Anthropologist* 11:11-22.

Lewis, T. M. N., 1943. Late Horizons in the Southeast. *Proceedings of the American Philosophical Society* 86:304-312.

--, 1953. Early Historic Cherokee Data. *Southeastern Archaeological Conference Newsletter* 3 (3):28-30.

Manucy, Albert C., 1962. *The Fort at Frederica*, The Department of Anthropology, Florida State University, Notes in Anthropology, No. 5 (Tallahassee).

Mason, Carole I., 1963. 18th Century Culture Change Among the Lower Creek. *Florida Anthropologist* 16 (3):65-81.

Morrell, L. Ross, 1965. *The Woods Island Site in Southeastern Acculturation 1625-1800*, The Department of Anthropology, Florida State University, Notes in Anthropology, No. 11 (Tallahassee).

Neitzel, Robert S., 1965. *Archaeology of the Fatherland Site: The Grand Village of the Natchez*, Anthropological Papers of the American Museum of Natural History, Vol. 51, Part 1 (New York).

Olsen, Stanley J., 1963. Dating Early Plain Buttons by their Form. *American Antiquity* 28:551-4.

Quimby, George I., 1957. *The Bayou Goula Site, Iberville Parish, Louisiana*, Fieldiana: Anthropology, Vol. 47, No. 2 (Chicago: Chicago Natural History Museum).

Sears, William H., 1955. Creek and Cherokee Culture in the 18th Century. *American Antiquity* 21:143-49.

--, 1964. The Southeastern United States. In *Prehistoric Man in the New World*, Jennings and Norbeck, eds. (Chicago: University of Chicago Press).

Smith, Hale G., 1956. *The European and the Indian,* Florida Anthropological Society Publications, No. 4 (Gainesville).

———————————, 1965. *Archaeological Excavations at Santa Rosa Pensacola,* The Department of Anthropology, Florida State University, Notes in Anthropology, No. 10 (Tallahassee).

Stephenson, Robert L., 1969. Archaeology at Charles Towne. The Institute of Archaeology and Anthropology, The University of South Carolina, *Notebook* 1(11):9-13.

Sturtevant, William C., 1962. Spanish-Indian Relations in Southeastern North America. *Ethnohistory* 9:41-108.

Swanton, John R., 1911. *Indian Tribes of the Lower Mississippi Valley and Adjacent Coast of the Gulf of Mexico.* Bureau of American Ethnology, Bulletin, No. 43 (Washington, D.C.: GPO).

———————————, 1928. *Social Organization and Social Usages of the Indians of the Creek Confederacy.* Bureau of American Ethnology, Annual Report, No. 42 (Washington, D.C.: GPO).

Trigger, Bruce G., 1968. *Beyond History: The Methods of Prehistory* (New York: Holt, Rinehart and Winston).

Willey, Gordon R., and William H. Sears, 1952. The Kasita Site. *Southern Indian Studies* 4:3-18.

Williams, Stephen, 1967. On the Location of the Historic Taensa Villages. *Conference on Historic Site Archaeology, Papers,* Stanley South, ed., Vol. 2, Part 1, pp. 2-13.

Witthoft, John, 1966. A History of Gunflints. *Pennsylvania Archaeologist* 36:12-49.

Comments

CHARLES H. FAIRBANKS

As a group these four papers are impressive as an inventory of what is known, what is unknown, and what ought to be known about the Indians and early history of the Southeastern United States. I was particularly impressed by the fact that each participant was able to summarize a great deal of information which was probably not familiar even to regional specialists in the specific disciplines. Each generation seems compelled to rediscover much of the work done by previous scholars. A significant function of such a symposium as this is to summarize and list the basic work, thus encouraging pathfinding in new fields. I believe that these four papers will provide this guidance.

Certainly no one is more capable of discussing Southeastern linguistics than Mary Haas. Her paper gives an admirable and thoughtful discussion, largely centered around the theme of linguistic diversity in the area and the history of attempts to classify the many languages there present. It was tantalizing to hear Haas speak of her widespread work in Tunica, Natchez, Creek, Koasati, Hitchiti, and Choctaw.

In talking of reconstructive studies, Haas is really speaking in part about glottochronology. She refers to Siebert's pioneering study (1967) using botanical and zoological terms to suggest the original homeland for the Proto-Algonkian people. Similar studies could be done for Muskogean and perhaps for Cherokee (Iroquoian). For the archeologist, the question is not that Iroquois and Cherokee are related, or that they evidently separated at a particular time, but whether the recovered archeological evidence supports, in detail, such a conclusion. I must confess that I cannot see that it does for Iroquois and Cherokee, which certainly doesn't question either the relationship or the time interval. What does interest me is how Cherokee early historic material, social, and religious cultural elements can relate so closely to their Muskogean counterparts with little or no evidence of linguistic relationship.

Can we but weave a fabric of linguistics, archaeology, ethnohistory, and physical anthropology that will contain these disparate observations, it may well resemble more a straight-jacket than a shopping bag, but the attempt should be made. Even more interesting would be a complex linguistic, ethnographic, and bioanthropological attack on the question of the homeland and migrations of the Muskogean peoples.

Louis De Vorsey's paper was a revelation to most of us of the resources provided by early maps, especially in the hands of such a skilled historical geographer. Most of us have consulted early maps, usually for the purpose of locating Indian villages. It is clear from De Vorsey's work that considerably greater information is available and that cooperation with geographers can be rewarding. The discussion of the Indian Boundary Line, and its delineation from a large series of medium scale local maps, represents a valuable basic document for Southeastern ethnohistorical studies. In addition, it suggests the values that might be derived from similar studies of the later treaty lines in the Southeast. These have been mapped in a general study (Royce 1902), but no detailed analysis of the lines is known to me. Would it be possible to study these treaty lines from the standpoint of conflicting Indian and Colonial concepts of resources and terrain? From the results indicated by De Vorsey, it would seem that such studies are possible and would be rewarding from a cultural standpoint.

The second part of this paper deals with the verification of the original forest cover from the original surveyors' maps. These plats were made when individual land holdings were established and should represent the original condition of the forest. The use of such data was completely new to me, although I had used the original federal survey field notes for the Territory of Florida in site survey and in attempts to locate Seminole communities. De Vorsey here suggests exciting possibilities for combined geographical and archeological studies. As he points out, surveyors generally note the species of trees, especially at corners. The biological scientists should be able, from this data, to reconstruct what resources were available in the specific area. Archaeological studies of food bones and plant remains in the Indian sites would give us an understanding of the local fauna used by the Indians. Up to the present our attempt to define the ecological niche for any aboriginal component has depended almost solely on either archeologic or documentary evidence. Never, as far as I am aware, has there been a coordination of the floral cover such as is suggested by De Vorsey's paper. Should pollen studies and analysis of archeological plant remains become commonly available, we might be able to make significant statements about the Indians' use of selected aspects of their environment.

Impressive as is David Hally's inventory of historic Indian archeology, I was impressed by the fact that unpublished theses and dissertations represent a much broader range of ethnic groups and time periods. It is clear that published materials are only a small part of what we know about the area. All anthropologists in the Southeast must continue to depend heavily on Dockstader's *The American Indian in Graduate Studies* (1957) which is supposed to be updated shortly. A great deal of work has been done which has not been formally published and a number of students are presently at work. Probably the best excavated historic site in the Southeast is Ocmulgee Old Fields on Ocmulgee National Monument. Yet the only significant report so far is in an unpublished dissertation (Mason 1963). There is clearly a need for greater dissemination of the large body of data that has been accumulating over the past forty years.

Hally properly calls attention to the increased precision of dating made possible by recent studies of historic European materials found on Indian sites. It seems clear that continued research, often related to the excavation of European settlements, will yield increased accuracy in these areas. I suspect that new methods of dating, such as thermoluminescence, will also allow us to be much more exact in our dating.

While Hally's discussion of the interaction of Spanish and Indian cultures very adequately summarizes the published literature, recent unpublished work must modify some of his conclusions. It seems to me that documentary and archeologic evidence agree that the mission system did indeed profoundly affect Indian culture. In both the Santa Fe area (modern Gainesville) and the Apalachee area (modern Tallahassee) profound changes are apparent. Most of the Potano and Apalachee sites of the 17th century are single component sites. At least for the Timucua area it is clear that the historic towns represent the end of a long cultural tradition. This Alachua tradition changes through time, yet represents continued evolution along well established trends. Yet the mission sites and Spanish cattle ranches have little stratigraphic depth. We know from documents that the priests tried to establish more permanent villages among their charges. The fact that these communities were built on new sites strongly suggests fundamental changes in the subsistance base. The presence of large quantities of peach pits at Fig Springs seems to be the only direct evidence we have as to the type of acculturation involved. I suspect that similar changes can be demonstrated for Apalachee, and perhaps for Guale.

The Creek and Cherokee areas showed comparable changes, although they seem to have been evoked by the pressures of the Indian trade system. So little seems to be known about the Chickasaw and Choctaw that I feel unsure about the situation in those areas.

Hally calls to our attention the very real needs in Southeastern historic Indian archeology. We certainly need more extensive, rather than intensive, excavations. Equally critical is a planned approach to problem oriented excavation of known towns. The direct historical approach will only work, it seems to me, if it deals with specifically identified sites. This implies a very extensive use of documents and close cooperation between historian, geographer, and archeologist. Hally's plea that the direct historical approach be applied to specific known towns seems to be entirely valid and promises worthwhile results. The implementation of such a program will necessarily involve abandonment of the present pattern of excavation where sites are chosen because of availability or because they are about to be destroyed. Systematic search, in documents and maps, for specific town locations must be followed by extensive excavations that will reveal community plan, burial complex, agricultural plots, and the entire recoverable culture complex. Only then can the archeologist begin to deal with the problems of Indian-European acculturation, community change, and ecological relationships. Without subscribing entirely to Wheeler's (1954) low opinion of stratigraphic test pitting, we have all known that it is primarily useful for establishing chronologies. We now have fairly secure chronologies for most of the major areas of the Southeast. Planned community excavation is long overdue. As far as I know, only Joffre Coe's recent attack on Cherokee origins represents such a systematic approach.

William Pollitzer's paper represents a valuable synthesis of the work so far done in physical anthropology in the Southeast. Like that of Mary Haas, it clearly shows the shift from broad regional, descriptive, classificatory approaches at an early period to specifically oriented functional problems. Once again I am impressed with the amount of material which has been published in recent years. I think that most of us find it difficult to keep up with current

literature outside of our own field and area. Papers such as these
serve a very useful summarizing purpose.

Pollitzer clearly shows, as did Haas especially, how the style
of research and writing has changed in a century or more. Now
much of the bio-anthropology is concerned with blood types and
characteristics that can be treated as monogenic traits. What has
been learned from these studies seems largely to confirm the linguistic,
ethnohistoric, and archeologic data which are available. I suspect
that it will take some time to satisfactorily project bio-anthropological
data back to the older archeological horizons. We do, however,
have a solid base on which to build at both ends of the sequences.
Pollitzer's recommendations for needed work are entirely sound, and
I hope that our current crops of graduate students will not become
so enamored with monkey-watching and other glamourous pursuits
as to see archeological bones only as examination problems. The body
of material is now sufficient so that meaningful studies should be
attempted.

These four papers give a comprehensive review of accomplish-
ments in Southeastern Indian studies. They present the first general
synthesis in many years, and the first ever to deal with the whole
range of studies. A truly satisfactory synthesis will require close
coordination between anthropologists and historians. Surely there
are historians who have been working in this field, even though they
may not be communicating freely with anthropologists. New
documents are coming to light, and long familiar ones are receiving
fresh scrutiny. The work of Malone with Cherokee sources is
highly useful (1956), as are Gearing's excellent papers (1962, 1958).
For the Creek area we have an excellent biography of the romantic
William Augustus Bowles (Wright 1967) and Cotterill's general
summary of the Southern frontier (1954) as well as a broad range of
more specific papers. For Florida and the Seminole there has been a
continued flow of papers led by the reprinting of many of the earlier
works by the University of Florida Press (Giddings, Latour, Cohen,
Sprague, Solis de Meras, Forbes, Ribaut).

Space will not permit even a listing of the forty books and
papers which have appeared during the past thirty years that have
made significant contributions to Seminole ethnography. It would
require a lengthy essay to comment in any significant way on them.
Here I can only indicate some of the trends that I see developing
since John R. Swanton's *Indians of the Southeastern United States*
(1946). Two main themes are characteristic of this new body of
work. One is the publication of original colonial or territorial docu-

ments not previously available. This includes scholarly editions with notes, such as Francis Harper's "Naturalists' Edition" of the *Travels of William Bartram* (1958). These publications include basic source material on the colonial period and for some later periods, especially the Second Seminole War in the 1830s. The major publication is, of course, the five volumes of the *Territorial Papers* edited by Carter (1956-1962). These cover the period 1821 to 1845 in considerable detail. In accord with the established policy for the *Territorial Papers*, they did not publish documents dealing solely with Indian affairs. There is, however, a good deal of Indian material in them and highly adequate footnotes indicate the reference data to a great deal more. These documents represent a major source for a study of Indian-white relations in the early years of the Territory.

A respectable body of newly published documents deal with the Spanish Colonial period. The Jesuit mission field in Florida has been amply documented in three works (Alegre, Zubillaga 1941; Zubillaga 1946). While one of these (Zubillaga 1946) is in Latin, they do present a massive collection of material on the early years of the Florida Colony. A very useful collection of Spanish maps is available which covers not only Florida but the more northern areas as well (Servicios . . . 1953). It is a fitting companion to Cumming's *Southeast in Early Maps*. A somewhat later series represents journals of individuals engaged in the Second Seminole War (Bemrose 1966; Mahon 1960; Sunderman 1953). While the material on Indians in any one of these accounts is rather scanty, they do represent a continued interest in the period. Somewhat later is Sturtevant's report on a trip through the Everglades by R. H. Pratt in 1879 (1956). As a whole these journals and accounts reveal a continued interest by historians and do add valuable data.

In the second realm are reports of recent ethnographic work, along with a few attempts at synthesis. Perhaps the most original contribution is Louis Capron's description of the existence of medicine bundles among the Seminole (1953). More specialized is Densmore's study of Seminole music (1956). Alexander Spoehr made a systematic study of Seminole kinship during the late thirties which gives us an exceptionally solid base to judge changes through time (1941a, 1941b, 1942, 1944). Ethel Cutler Freeman has been working for a number of years among the Seminole and has made a number of valuable observations, among which her studies of cultural change are especially interesting (1960, 1965). Specific studies of particular aspects of Seminole culture have been covered in a large number of papers over the last forty years. To mention only a few, out of several dozen, will give some indication of the sort of work that has been done. There has been an excellent study of Seminole patchwork men's clothing that describes in precise detail how this complex style is made (Anonymous 1959). Additional studies deal with medicine (Greenlee 1944), Osceola's coats (Sturtevant 1956), and silverwork (Goggin 1940). More comprehensive treatments are available which approach regional summaries or tribal syntheses. Sturtevant has published a thoughtful analysis of Spanish and Indian relations in the Southeast (1962). Goggin developed the beginning of a comprehensive classification of style areas in the Southeast (1952). Goggin and Sturtevant have collected a comprehensive body of data about the complexity of Calusa social-political organization, recognizing that it appears to have been of the ramage type (1964). Unfortunately there is no really modern synthesis of Seminole culture. McReynolds (1957) is largely a political study of individual events and largely concerned with the Oklahoma bands. The Indian Claims Commission studies have resulted in a comprehensive study of Seminole origins (Fairbanks 1957) which can now be revised and published. In spite of all this ethnohistorical work, we really need comprehensive summaries of the major tribes of the Southeast, and the material is available if someone can but find the time to synthesize it.

REFERENCES

Alegre, Francisco Javier, 1960. Historia de la provincia de la Compania de Jesus de Nueva Espana, Tomo IV, libros 9-10 (Anos 1676-1766), Nueva edicion por Ernest J. Burrus y Felix Zubillaga. *Bibliotheca Instituti Historici,* S.J., Vol. 17, Rome.

Anonymous, 1959. Seminole Patchwork. *American Indian Hobbyist* 6:3-18.

Bemrose, John, 1966. *Reminiscences of the Second Seminole War,* John K. Mahon, ed. (Gainesville: University of Florida Press).

Capron, Louis, 1953. *The Medicine Bundles of the Florida Seminole and the Green Corn Dance.* Smithsonian Institution, Bureau of American Ethnology Anthropological Paper No. 35, Bulletin 151 (Washington, D.C.: GPO), pp. 159-210.

Carter, Clarence Edwin, ed., 1956-1962. *The Territorial Papers of the United States: The Territory of Florida,* Vols. 22-26 (Washington: The National Archives).

Cohen, M. M., 1964. *Notices of Florida and the Campaigns.* Reprint of the 1836 edition, O. Z. Tyler, Jr., ed. (Gainesville: University of Florida Press).

Cotterill, R. S., 1954. *The Southern Indians: The Story of the Civilized Tribes before Removal* (Norman: University of Oklahoma Press).

Densmore, Frances, 1956. *Seminole Music.* Smithsonian Institution, Bureau of American Ethnology Bulletin 161 (Washington, D.C.: GPO).

Dockstader, Frederick J., 1957. *The American Indian in Graduate Studies: A Bibliography of Theses and Dissertations.* Contributions from the Museum of the American Indian, Heye Foundation, Vol. XV (New York).

Fairbanks, Charles H., 1957. *Ethnological Report, Florida Seminole.* 300 pp. mimeographed manuscript

74   *Red, White, and Black*

Forbes, James Grant, 1964. *Sketches, Historical and Topographical, of the Floridas,* Reprint of the 1821 edition, James W. Covington, ed. (Gainesville: University of Florida Press).

Freeman, Ethel Cutler, 1960. Culture stability and change among the Seminoles of Florida. In *Selected papers of the 5th International Congress of Anthropological and Ethnological Sciences* (Philadelphia), pp. 249-254.

————, 1965. Two Types of Cultural Response to External Pressures Among the Florida Seminole. *Anthropological Quarterly* 38: 55-61.

Gearing, Fred, 1958. The Structural Poses of 18th Century Cherokee Villages. *American Anthropologist* 60:1148-1157.

————, 1962. *Priests and Warriors: Social Structures for Cherokee Politics in the 18th Century.* American Anthropological Association, Memoir 93 (Menasha, Wisconsin).

Giddings, Joshua R., 1964. *The Exiles of Florida,* Reprint of 1858 edition, Emmett B. Peter, Jr., ed. (Gainesville: University of Florida Press).

Goggin, J. M., 1940. Silverwork of the Florida Seminole. *El Palacio* 47(2): 25-32.

————, 1952. Style Areas in Historic Southeastern Art. In *Indian Tribes of Aboriginal America,* Vol. III, Proceedings, 29th Congress of Americanists (Chicago: University of Chicago Press), pp. 172-176.

Goggin, J. M., and W. C. Sturtevant, 1964. The Calusa: A Stratified, Nonagricultural Society (with notes on Sibling marriage). In *Explorations in Cultural Anthropology,* Ward H. Goodenough, ed. (New York: McGraw-Hill), pp. 179-219.

Greenlee, Robert F., 1944. Medicine and Curing Practices of the Modern Florida Seminoles. *American Anthropologist* 46:317-328.

Harper, Francis, ed., 1958. *The Travels of William Bartram,* Naturalist's Edition (New Haven: Yale University Press).

Latour, A. L., 1964. *Historical Memoir of the War in West Florida and Louisiana in 1814-15,* Reprint of the 1816 edition, Jane Lucas de Grammond, ed. (Gainesville: University of Florida Press).

Mahon, John K., 1960. The Journal of A. B. Meek and the Second Seminole War, 1836. *Florida Historical Quarterly* 38:302-18.

Malone, Henry T., 1956. *Cherokees of the Old South: A People in Transition.* (Athens: University of Georgia Press).

Mason, Carol Irwin, 1963. The Archaeology of Ocmulgee Old Fields, Macon, Georgia. Unpublished Ph.D. diss., University of Michigan.

McReynolds, Edwin C., 1957. *The Seminoles.* Civilization of the American Indian Series (Norman, Oklahoma: University of Oklahoma Press).

Ribaut, Jean, 1964. *The Whole and True Discoverye of Terra Florida,* Reprint of the 1563 edition, David L. Dowd, ed. (Gainesville: University of Florida Press).

Royce, Charles C., 1902. *Indian Land Cessions in the United States.* Bureau of American Ethnology, 18th Annual Report, Part 2. (Washington, D.C.: GPO).

Servicios Geografico e Historico del Ejercito. 1949. Cartografia de Ultramar. Carpeta I. America en General, Madrid. 1953. Carpeta II. Estados Unidos y Canada, Toponimia de los Mapas que la Integran Relaciones de Ultramar, Madrid.

Solis de Meras, Gonzalo, 1967. *Pedro Menendez de Aviles,* Reprint of the Florida State Historical Society edition, Lyle N. McAlister, ed. (Gainesville: University of Florida Press).

Spoehr, Alexander, 1941a. Camp, Clan, and Kin Among the Cow Creek Seminole. *Anthropological Series, Field Museum of Natural History,* 33.

————, 1941b. "Friends" Among the Seminole. *The Chronicle of Oklahoma* 19:252.

————————————, 1942. Kinship System of the Seminole. *Anthropological Series*, Field Museum of Natural History, 33 (2): 31-113.

————————————, 1944. The Florida Seminole Camp. *Anthropological Series*, Field Museum of Natural History 33 (3):117-150.

Sprague, John T., 1964. *The Origin, Progress, and Conclusion of the Florida War*, Reprint of the 1848 edition, John K. Mahon, ed. (Gainesville: University of Florida Press).

Sturtevant, William C., 1956. R. H. Pratt's Report on the Seminole in 1879. *Florida Anthropologist* 9:1-24.

————————————, 1956. Osceola's Coats? *Florida Historical Quarterly* 34: 315-328.

————————————, 1962. Spanish-Indian Relations in Southeastern North America. *Ethnohistory* 9:41-94.

Sunderman, J. F., ed., 1953. *Journey into Wilderness; an Army Surgeon's Account of Life in Camp and Field During Creek and Seminole Wars, 1836-1838* (Gainesville: University of Florida Press).

Swanton, John R., 1946. *The Indians of the Southeastern United States*. Bureau of American Ethnology, Bulletin 137 (Washington, D.C.: GPO).

Wheeler, Sir Mortimer, 1954. *Archaeology from the Earth* (Baltimore: Penguin Books).

Wright, J. Leitch, Jr., 1967. *William Augustus Bowles: Director General of the Creek Nation* (Athens: University of Georgia Press).

Zubillaga, Felix, 1946. Monumenta Antiquae Floridae (1566-1572), *Monumenta Historic Societatis, Iesu,* (Roma).

————————————, 1941. La Florida La Mision Jesuitica (1566-1572) y La Colonization Espanola. Bibliotheca Instituti Historici S.I., Roma, Institutum Historicum S.I.

Part II

The Ante-Bellum Elite

F. N. Boney

The upper class whites of the ante-bellum South have been dissected and examined by a host of scholars, but they remain veiled by time and distorted by legend. This relatively small fraternity of the elite was composed of a complicated conglomerate of people bound together by blood and land, marriage and money, tradition and necessity, but the essence of this fluid class was the planter, and he too remains an elusive historical figure. He could be a dignified, slightly seedy Tidewater Virginian, proud of his ancient and honorable lineage (all two or three generations of it) and content to sell enough crops to meet normal expenses and enough surplus slaves to pay for a burst of grand living or an overdue debt. Or he could be a rough and ready pioneer on the rich, virgin land along the Mississippi River, living in a crude cabin in the midst of vast fields of cotton and large gangs of black workers. The vague term planter encompassed a bewildering array of actual people, but basically the planter was an agriculturist with much land and many slaves, say twenty or, better still, say a large number which included at least twenty able-bodied field hands (Stampp 1956: 28-31; Randall and Donald 1969: 39-41).[1]

There really was no such thing as an "average" planter, not within a culture which encouraged individualism and tolerated eccentricity, but most of these diverse fellows were much closer to the Mississippi hustler than the Virginia mandarin.[2] The planter of the Old South was fundamentally a businessman, an American capitalist investing his resources for a profit, a thoroughgoing materialist as attracted to the fast buck as any Yankee. Early writers usually placed the planter in a very unique, isolated compartment of American and even Southern life, bequeathing a blurred, distorted image to the future, and ironically some modern scholarship is swinging back full cycle toward this old view, especially the ante-bellum view of the planter as a genteel, hospitable, impetuous pleasure seeker who was indifferent to money matters and often ineffectual in a crisis (Genovese 1965:13-36 and 1969; Weaver 1968; Randall and Donald 1969:44; Stampp 1956:43; Atherton 1949:7-8; Elkins 1963:27-80; Taylor 1961).

The planter belongs in the broad mainstream of ante-bellum American society. He cannot be shuttled off into some feudal or seigneurial or nonmaterialistic or precapitalistic world which is not only gone with the wind but never really existed in any meaningful manner. The white master of many black slaves was obviously different to some degree from other southerners and other Americans but not nearly different enough to be placed in a rigidly separate social and cultural compartment. Basically the planter was an agricultural entrepreneur, well within the general context of American capitalism.[8] The upper class Southerner was not nearly as different from other Americans, North and South, as he is often portrayed. He never was and still is not (Cash 1961:36-37, 41-43; Phillips 1964:165; Owsley 1969:34-37; Craven 1939:63-97; Boney 1969:372-74).

The planter's general attitude toward Indians and Negroes was not out of the mainstream of white American thought either. America was a white man's country, North and South, and neither reds nor blacks really "fitted in" properly. These people were too different, too untypical to fit into the kind of neat, tidy cultural package Americans have always sought but only recently come even close to attaining. The Indians inhabited large areas of the South, including farmlands; white planters and farmers wanted this land for their own agricultural enterprises. One way or another the Indian and his ways had to be removed from the path of the American juggernaut called progress. The Negro was a greater abomination, an even more inferior being fit only to hew wood and draw water for his betters under some sort of strict social control; the greater the percentage of blacks, the more severe the control. These sentiments were shared by "true" (that is, white) Americans of every class in all sections of the country (Litwack 1961; Hagan 1961; Jordan 1969: 414-15).

The concentration of black slave labor in the South and the tendency of the frontier to linger there too stimulated the development of more intense feelings within the general white American consensus, but, then as now, the Southerner was not beyond this consensus but only in the vocal forefront of it. White Southerners spoke out louder and clearer than most Americans when they discussed ethnic minorities, but basically they said what other Americans believed. They reflected—and still reflect—with considerable candor the passions and prejudices of the great American folk. Throughout our history the vocal white Southerner has unwittingly given the American people a free look into their own souls. No greater outrage can be committed than to make a whole tribe or folk see themselves accurately; men have been crucified or burned or gassed or shot for this sort of cultural treason. The Southern people have only suffered a kind of exile (Craven 1939:63-97; Zinn 1964:262-63; Boney 1966:246-47).[4]

The ante-bellum planter has been exiled or isolated the most, for his large, direct stake in slavery, his insatiable land-lust, and his relative articulateness made him the most visible element within Southern society. Poor whites were highly visible—travelers like Frederick Law Olmsted did not miss a one—but largely muted. The massive Southern middle class spoke out well enough but was either ignored—it did not exist so how could it speak?—or mistaken for the elite. Well qualified in some respects, the confident planter spoke out loud and clear on the Indian and Negro questions (Owsley 1969:30-32; Olmsted 1959; Eaton 1961:18-19).

Probably the Southern elite's most idealistic, thoughtful spokesman on these matters was Thomas Jefferson, as good a man and as fine a mentality as this class ever produced. In his classic *Notes on the State of Virginia*, written in the 1780s, Jefferson warned that in judging blacks, "The opinion that they are inferior in the faculties of reason and imagination, must be hazarded with great diffidence." (1964:138). Yet in this same work he did hazard this basic opinion openly, even relentlessly, not hesitating a few pages earlier to refer to "the real distinctions which nature has made" (1964:132) and to point out proofs that "their inferiority is not the effect merely of their condition of life" (1964:136).

To Jefferson black was ugly, an aesthetic error by nature. He felt that Negroes were excessively lustful and inadequately reflective. Jefferson was willing to concede that in memory blacks were equal to whites—an occasional divergence from the general consensus is to be expected of a radical like "Mad Tom"—but he had no real doubt of their inferior powers of reason: "I think one could scarcely be found capable of tracing and comprehending the investigations of Euclid" (1964:134).[5] He also thought that blacks had deficient imaginations which left them relatively barren in the fine arts (with the traditional exception of music). Basically Jefferson suspected —really believed—"that the blacks . . . are inferior to the whites in the endowments both of body and mind" (1964:138). Theoretically he favored emancipation of the slaves, but he insisted that it had to be accompanied by a policy of removal. White society had to be purged not only of slavery but also of black people. Thirty years after Jefferson's death, when a new political party emerged with the determination to keep the western territories free of slavery (and, to be truthful, of Negroes too), it was only appropriate that it should reach back, borrow the worn banners of the Jeffersonians, and call itself the Republican Party (Jefferson 1964:132-38; Jordan 1969:435-40; Litwack 1961:269-72).

The master of Monticello (and of more than 200 slaves) had a very different view of Indians. This picture is not clear and concise, for the red man in his pure form was always somewhat shadowy, even for a young man who grew up near the frontier. Completely unlike the black man, the Indian was a free creature usually beyond the white man's pale. To Jefferson, Indians were brave, virile, and attractive, not the equal of the whites in their current environment, but, unlike the blacks, capable of improvement and even equality with the whites under the proper circumstances. He marveled at their natural talents in art and oratory which proved "their reason and sentiment strong, their imagination glowing and elevated" (1964:135). Jefferson so admired the red man that he, like his early mentor Patrick Henry, even speculated on the happy prospect of intermarriage between reds and whites and the evolution of a splendid new kind of American. This was the very opposite of his attitude toward blacks, a people he was convinced could never be properly absorbed into the white majority (Jefferson 1964:88-94, 134-5; Jordan 1969:163, 177-81).

Jefferson's overall image of the Negro was fairly standard. This son of the Enlightenment was learned and eloquent, and the cutting edge of his criticisms was slightly blunted by idealism and humanitarianism, but, even so, basically he stated what most other white Americans thought and said much more crudely—the Negro was inferior, debased beyond redemption. Put in the common vernacular most of his basic attitude was acceptable even to "rednecks," "peckerwoods," and other exotic variations of the lowest classes of Southern whites. His view of the Indian was less typical. Whites generally rated Indians higher than Negroes, but Jefferson not only blunted his criticisms of red men but shifted to outright praise in many instances. The image of the Indian was always complex and contradictory, allowing for considerable divergency of opinion among whites. Perhaps Mother Virginia had mellowed more than most areas as the red menace faded to the west. Some "First Families of Virginia," ever conscious of blood lines in people and horses, were (and still are) proud of an Indian forebearer—always nobility like Pocahontas, of course, and not just any run-of-the-wilderness red. Or perhaps the "noble savage" image which was so powerful and persuasive in literary circles made Jefferson more sympathetic to Indians than his less intellectual contemporaries, which included most planters as well as the masses (Phillips 1964:151-65; Sheehan 1969:327-59).[6]

Whatever the reason, Jefferson's view of the Indian was too favorable for most Americans. More typical, although slightly to the hostile side of the mainstream this time, was writer-planter Joseph B. Cobb, a native of Oglethorpe County, Georgia, who migrated to Mississippi. He thought Indians were as degraded as black slaves and besides "noted for cowardice, and craft, and meanness of every description" (Cobb 1851:156-78). He detected no nobility or virtue at all, and in some respects he found blacks, especially native Africans, more interesting and admirable, the red man's superior in every way.[7] The Choctaw and Chickasaw, the tribes he knew best, were beneath contempt, that is, even worse than black slaves (Cobb 1851:176-78; Rogers 1969:131-46).

Certainly many planters, without agreeing with Jefferson, were considerably more lenient in their appraisals of Indians. Even an old Indian killer like Andrew Jackson occasionally showed some sympathy for the red man, but he was certainly no admirer of the Indian's "erratic" way of life or of red military power, and his official removal policy still speaks louder than an occasional moderate utterance (Prucha 1969:527-39).[8] Cobb and Jackson more accurately represented planter attitudes toward Indians than did Jefferson, but all three would have agreed with most Americans on the hopeless inferiority of blacks (Davis 1969:286). Reduced to the slogans so dear to our own culture, planters could have put it this way: Good Indian = Long-Gone Indian, Good Negro = Sambo Slave.

Planter attitudes toward reds and blacks were particularly important because this elite class exercised great power within the Old South, power out of all proportion to its meager numbers. Even after the triumph of Jacksonian Democracy—that is, equal rights for all adult white males—this elite still maintained great influence. The white masses were not overawed by the planters—they knew them too well for that—but they did often turn to their prosperous, prominent neighbors for guidance and leadership. Never in American history has one small aristocratic group exercised such disproportionate power for so long. And never in American history did such a leadership group fail so disastrously.

Relatively poised and polished on the surface but confused and contorted within, the planter elite encouraged the South to defy several significant trends in western civilization, trends which had gathered considerable momentum early in the onrushing nineteenth century. Tenaciously defending and expanding an economy based on large-scale, commercial agriculture which was in turn based on black slave labor, the elite championed a way of life which, while by no means isolated from the mainstream of western civilization, did, especially in regard to slavery, challenge some powerful new currents within that mainstream. The Southern white masses cannot escape much responsibility for this suicidal strategy, but their greatest blunder was to allow an entrenched elite too much influence. Or, to put it rather bluntly, too often the yeoman masses followed elite asses (Craven 1939:78-80, 89-91; Owsley 1969:39-41; Randall and Donald 1969:37-49; Craven 1953:252-65; Davidson 1961:68-75; Mannix and Cowley 1965:263-87; Freehling 1968:49-86; Eaton 1964:35).[9]

History is not entirely inevitable, men are not powerless ciphers, and leaders can influence events. Change, especially reform, always comes hard, but it is almost always possible. Decay and disaster were not predestined for the Old South, but the Southern elite, the traditional leadership cadre, could not or would not fashion the necessary reform. From the beginning when slavery evolved in seventeenth century Virginia, the planters (and would-be planters) encouraged the expansion of this peculiar institution which was the foundation of their prosperity—or at least seemed to be. The traditional Christian opposition to enslaving fellow Christians faded rapidly as blacks were converted—as usual in such eyeball-to-eyeball confrontations between God and man, God blinked first. And very soon appeared the slave codes, Sambo Statutes which debased a whole race. Every colonial appeal for a cessation of the importation of slaves during hard times was balanced by pleas for more slaves when crop prices were good and land was plentiful (Davis 1969:136-44, 197-211, 244-54; Jordan 1969:71-82; Franklin 1963:70-3).

If Indians possessed such land, they were usually muscled aside, but occasionally they were more useful unmolested. Virginia and Carolina planters involved in the extensive fur trade found cooperation with certain tribes quite profitable. Especially in South Carolina white leadership was sometimes able to play the blacks and reds off against each other effectively. Some planters felt that nearby Indians

intimidated and pacified restless blacks, but this was always an un-
predictable policy. As Andrew Jackson said, Indians were "erratic."
They were not always reliable allies in the onward and upward
march of white civilization. After the long, bloody second Seminole
War of 1835-1842, planters could never be sure that neighboring
Indians would not absorb runaway blacks into their own orbit and
enlist them as allies in resistance to white aggression. Certainly white
troopers who had faced the fury of red and black Seminole warriors
would have expressed considerable doubt about using red men to
control black men for the benefit of white men (Porter 1964:427-40;
Hagan 1961:76-7; Morton 1960 [1]:227-55; Willis 1963:157-76).

In the long, grim history of Southern slavery there was never a
significant, meaningful movement to free the blacks in a single
Southern state, and the planter class, so often portrayed as the
spearhead of Southern enlightenment, certainly failed to lead wisely
or really to lead at all in this sensitive area. Even in mellow old
Virginia emancipation never made any significant progress, not before
the Civil War nor before the abolition crusade nor even during the
golden age of Jeffersonian liberalism. And aging Jefferson himself,
in the twilight of a glorious career, with little to lose politically and
everything to gain historically, avoided the hard but vital task.
Like lesser planters, his whole life was inextricably entangled with
slavery, and he was in some ways as trapped as his field hands.
The closest Virginia ever came to serious action was the dramatic
legislative session following Nat Turner's uprising, a "fire bell in
the night" if there ever was one. However, even then the reformers
failed as the planter elite lined up massively on the side of the status
quo. The picture is no better in the rest of the upper South and
much worse in the real "land of cotton." A few upper class Southerners—a James G. Birney in Alabama and Kentucky, a Grimké
in South Carolina, a Clay (Cassius Marcellus or Henry) in Kentucky
—did try for some reform, but, overall, the planters were no more
interested in real reform than the white masses (Cohen 1969:503-26;
Robert 1941; Eaton 1966:350; McColley 1964; Sellers 1960: 40-71).[10]

Worse yet, upper class Southerners spearheaded a counter crusade
to convince the Southern people (perhaps themselves most of all)
that slavery was a positive good. Novelist Nathaniel Beverley Tucker,
politician John C. Calhoun, minister Leonidas Polk, professor Thomas
R. Dew, agriculturist Edmund Ruffin, scientist Josiah Nott, and a
host of other elitists proclaimed the glad tidings. Many of this same
class also championed the final great crusade, political separation
from a Union increasingly less friendly toward slavery. The Southern

masses were not really tricked or conned; the Old South's last disastrous decisions were reasonably democratic; but certainly in the final crises the planter elite demonstrated insufficient vision and wisdom (Eaton 1966:344-51; Craven 1953:349-401; Catton 1961:130-215; Randall and Donald 1969:85-90 and 135-41).

Within the overall leadership failure of the planter elite, special attention should be paid to the total failure of their women. The aristocratic ladies of the Old South were a super elite, the very cream of what is still sometimes referred to as "pure white Southern womanhood". Seldom has a group been so honored in word and so ignored in deed. The planter's praise for his women—and indeed all Southern white women—was so overwhelming that it continues to bemuse many observers. Even a skeptic like W. J. Cash was misled by the rhetoric when he declared that the rebel army charged into battle convinced it was fighting wholly for HER (1961:89). Alas, for every such chivalrous cavalier there was probably at least one Johnny Reb who marched into combat in order to get that much farther away from a nagging wife and a half dozen bawling brats (Eaton 1966:396-407).

Still, Southern women, and especially Southern upper class ladies, did have superficial prestige and thus some influence. They were not in a position to gain special knowledge of the Indian, but they did suffer superior insights into the grim reality of slavery. The vulnerability of black women, the helplessness of black men, the power and passion of white men, the inevitable mulatto children, the plantation lady knew the whole story—and did nothing. They gossiped surely and occasionally confided to their diaries, but they *did* nothing until the Civil War finally came. Then these gentle-women sent their men off to a slaughter which would leave many of them embittered widows and spinsters, old "aunties" passing their hatreds and frustrations on to new generations (Catton 1967:400-3; Thomas 1968:396-401; Chesnut 1961:2-43; Boney 1969:35-6, 48-9; Eaton 1965:87-89).

The Civil War marked the bloody end of the Old South, and it was altogether appropriate that an aristocrat, Jefferson Davis, should preside over this last, greatest debacle. No better symbol could be found for a lost cause than the distinguished planter from Mississippi. Intelligent and patriotic, experienced in war and politics, brave and determined, he was the best the Southern elite had to offer in 1861—and he was inadequate. He was too aloof and reserved to fire a people who needed passionate leadership. He was too conservative at a time when daring chances had to be taken. He was a bumbling bureaucrat who failed to properly mobilize the South's meager resources. Like his aristocratic field commander, Robert E. Lee, he was good enough to prolong a war which exterminated more than 600,000 young Americans, but he was not good enough to win it (Potter 1968:263-86; Wiley 1968:1-42).[11]

President Davis did realize quickly that the Southern army would be greatly outnumbered, and, drawing upon his experience with western Indians while Secretary of War in the 1850s, he tried hard to recruit Indian soldiers. Working primarily with former Southern tribes which still held some slaves, he negotiated nine separate treaties with Creek, Cherokee, Choctaw, Chickasaw, and Seminole groups which for once gained significant concessions. Like white Americans the Indians were divided, and neither North nor South used red troops extensively. At the battle of Pea Ridge as many as 3,500 red rebels fought, and a few collected a scalp or two, but the Confederates still did not win that rather important western clash (Eaton 1965:49; Hagan 1961:99-103).

Davis, like an earlier planter named Jefferson, saw a vast difference between red men and black men. He spared no effort to recruit a few Indians, but he adamantly refused to even consider recruiting soldiers from the immense Southern black manpower pool. Even the North with its vast white population began to use black troops by the middle of the war, and by 1865 the Union army had recruited almost 200,000 blacks, mostly ex-slaves, that is, Southerners. Only in the very last months of the war, when defeat was inevitable, did it finally dawn on Davis and Lee and the other Southern aristocrats who prided themselves on knowing the Negro that black troops could have saved the Confederacy.[12] The rebel leaders retained their racial misconceptions to the bitter end—and beyond (Cornish 1966; Roland 1962:183-85; Eaton 1965:265).

The upper class of the Old South misjudged and mistreated the Indian and the Negro, but so did the rest of white America. When confronted with the same racial challenge, white Americans of every class and every section react very similarly. Indeed the wounds of the Civil War were not truly healed until white America closed ranks to resume its aggression against the Indian and its degradation of the Negro. The planter elite was soon back on top again, and in cooperation with its new urban-business allies it continues to exercise powerful influence in what is now called the New South. Hopefully upper class Southerners are finally ready, willing, *and* able to give consistently enlightened leadership to a region once again in considerable turmoil. After three centuries, it's about time (Faulkner 1959:6-8; Woodward 1951:211-15; Buck 1937).

NOTES

1. In this paper the term planter is used to designate men who cultivated large areas of land with gangs of slave laborers. It is not used in the colonial sense to designate anyone who cultivated the land from humblest farmer to the haughtiest grandee.

2. Of course, there were many agricultural hustlers in Virginia and by the 1850s some mandarins in Mississippi. Everywhere in the Old South the hustler outnumbered the mandarin by a large majority.

3. Any attempt to examine and evaluate the economy of the Old South usually boils down to an attempt to define capitalism as opposed to other economic systems. This often leads to a great deal of defining and very little describing.

4. Whether non-Southern Americans really think Southern whites are all that different or whether they consciously refuse to admit their own Southernism is difficult to determine. In such matters the mind of the North is inscrutable.

5. Jefferson's rampant "radicalism" is further evidenced by his sympathy for thieving slaves whose very freedom had been stolen. He also conceded that blacks were "at least as brave, and more adventuresome" than whites, but he added that this was perhaps the result of lack of foresight (Jefferson 1964:133-34).

6. As Alexander Hamilton and recent scholars like William T. Hagan and Leonard W. Levy have indicated, Saint Thomas was capable of duplicity on occasion. Under pressure he was willing to muscle the "noble savage" beyond the westward horizon.

7. Cobb had some interest in the culture and language of these native Africans, and, even more unusual, he had considerable respect for them. His description of the difference between these true Africans and native American slaves is an impressive illustration of the brutal, degrading effect of slavery on Negroes. The process Stanley M. Elkins calls infantilization is here documented by a Southerner who was staunchly defending the institution of slavery.

8. F. P. Prucha makes a good case for a more lenient evaluation of Jackson's Indian policies, but he puts a little too much stress on Jackson's words as opposed to his actions.

9. It is unwise to directly connect the rise of Jacksonian Democracy and the increase of racism in the United States (Davis 1969:286). The image of the wise, enlightened aristocrat restraining the reckless, racist masses is quite misleading—then or now.

10. A few maverick planters with liberal tendencies are often given much greater historical coverage than the overwhelming mass of conservative and even reactionary planters.

11. For a more sympathetic evaluation of Jefferson Davis see Frank E. Vandiver, *Their Tattered Flags: The Epic of the Confederacy* (New York and Evanston: Harper's Magazine Press, 1970).

12. In January 1864 Confederate General Patrick Cleburne suggested recruiting slaves into the rebel ranks, but the Confederate government rejected his controversial plan. Ten months later Cleburne was killed leading his troops in a headlong attack at Franklin, Tennessee.

REFERENCES

Atherton, Lewis E., 1949. *The Southern Country Store: 1800-1860* (Baton Rouge, Louisiana: Louisiana State University Press).

Boney, F. N., 1966. *John Letcher of Virginia: The Story of Virginia's Civil War Governor* (University, Alabama: University of Alabama Press).
————, 1969. Look Away, Look Away: A Distant View of Dixie. *Georgia Review* 23:368-74.
Buck, Paul H., 1937. *The Road to Reunion: 1865-1900* (Boston: Little Brown).
Cash, W. J., 1961. *The Mind of the South* (New York: Vintage of Random House). First published in 1941.
Catton, Bruce, 1961. *The Coming Fury* (Garden City, New York: Doubleday & Co.).
Chesnut, Mary Boykin, 1961. *A Diary from Dixie* (Cambridge, Massachusetts: Sentry of Houghton Mifflin Company). First published in 1905.
Cobb, Joseph B., 1851. *Mississippi Scenes; Or, Sketches of Southern and Western Life and Adventure, Humorous, Satirical, and Descriptive, Including the Legend of Black Creek* (Philadelphia: A. Hart, Late Carey & Hart).
Cohen, William, 1969. Thomas Jefferson and the Problem of Slavery. *Journal of American History* 56:503-26.
Cornish, Dudley Taylor, 1966. *The Sable Arm: Negro Troops in the Union Army, 1861-1865* (New York: W. W. Norton & Company). First published in 1956.
Craven, Avery, 1939. *The Repressible Conflict: 1830-1861* (Baton Rouge: Louisiana State University Press).
————, 1953. *The Growth of Southern Nationalism: 1848-1861* (Baton Rouge: Louisiana State University Press).
Davidson, Basil, 1961. *The African Slave Trade: Precolonial History: 1450-1850* (Boston: Atlantic Press of Little, Brown and Co.). Published in hardcover edition as *Black Mother*.
Davis, David Brion, 1969. *The Problem of Slavery in Western Culture* (Ithaca, New York: Cornell University Press). First published in 1966.
Eaton, Clement, 1961. *The Growth of Southern Civilization: 1790-1860* (New York: Harper & Bros.).
————, 1964. *The Freedom-of-Thought Struggle in the Old South* (New York: Harper Torchbooks of Harper & Row).
————, 1965. *A History of the Southern Confederacy* (New York: Free Press of Collier-Macmillan). First published in 1954.
————, 1966. *A History of the Old South* (New York: Macmillan Co.).
Elkins, Stanley M., 1963. *Slavery: A Problem in American Institutional and Intellectual Life* (New York: Grosset & Dunlap). First published in 1959.
Faulkner, Harold U., 1959. *Politics, Reform and Expansion: 1890-1900* (New York: Harper and Bros.).
Franklin, John Hope, 1963. *From Slavery to Freedom: A History of American Negroes* (New York: Alfred A. Knopf).
Freehling, William W., 1968. *Prelude to Civil War: The Nullification Controversy in South Carolina: 1816-1836* (New York: Harper Torchbooks of Harper & Row). First published in 1965.
Genovese, Eugene D., 1965. *The Political Economy of Slavery: Studies in the Economy and Society of the Slave South* (New York: Pantheon Books).
————, 1969. *The World the Slaveholders Made* (New York: Pantheon Books).
Hagan, William T., 1961. *American Indians* (Chicago: University of Chicago Press).
Jefferson, Thomas, 1964. *Notes on the State of Virginia* (New York: Harper Torchbooks of Harper & Row). First published in 1785.
Jordan, Winthrop D., 1969. *White Over Black: American Attitudes Toward the Negro: 1550-1812* (Baltimore: Penguin Books). First published in 1968.

Litwack, Leon F., 1961. *North of Slavery: The Negro in the Free States, 1790-1860* (Chicago: University of Chicago Press).

McColley, Robert, 1964. *Slavery and Jeffersonian Virginia* (Urbana, Illinois: University of Illinois Press).

Mannix, Daniel P. and Malcolm Cowley, 1965. *Black Cargoes: A History of the Atlantic Slave Trade: 1518-1865* (New York: Viking Press of Macmillan Co.). First published in 1962.

Morton, Richard L., 1960. *Colonial Virginia*, vol. 1 (Chapel Hill: University of North Carolina Press).

Olmsted, Frederick Law, 1959. *The Slave States* (New York: Capricorn Books).

Owsley, Harriet Chappell, ed., 1969. *The South: Old and New Frontiers: Selected Essays of Frank Lawrence Owsley* (Athens: University of Georgia Press).

Phillips, Ulrich Bennell, 1964. *The Course of the South to Secession* (New York: Hill and Wang). First published in 1939.

Porter, Kenneth W., 1964. Negroes and the Seminole War, 1835-1842. *Journal of Southern History* 30:427-40.

Potter, David M., 1968. *The South and the Sectional Conflict* (Baton Rouge: Louisiana State University Press).

Prucha, F. P., 1969. Andrew Jackson's Indian Policy: A Reassessment. *Journal of American History* 56:527-39.

Randall, J. G. and David Donald, 1969. *The Civil War and Reconstruction* (Lexington, Massachusetts: D. C. Heath and Co.).

Robert, Joseph Clark, 1941. *The Road from Monticello: A Study of the Virginia Slavery Debate of 1832* (Durham, North Carolina: Duke University Press).

Roland, Charles P., 1962. *The Confederacy* (Chicago: University of Chicago Press).

Rogers, Tommy W., 1969. Joseph B. Cobb: Antebellum Humorist and Critic. *Mississippi Quarterly* 22:131-46.

Sellers, Charles Grier, 1960. *The Southerner As American* (Chapel Hill: University of North Carolina Press).

Sheehan, Bernard W., 1969. Paradise and the Noble Savage in Jeffersonian Thought. *William and Mary Quarterly* 26:327-59.

Stampp, Kenneth M., 1956. *The Peculiar Institution: Slavery in the Ante-Bellum South* (New York: Alfred A. Knopf).

Taylor, William R., 1961. *Cavalier and Yankee: The Old South and American National Character* (New York: George Braziller, Inc.).

Thomas, Lately, 1968. *The First President Johnson: The Three Lives of the Seventeenth President of the United States of America* (New York: William Morrow & Co.).

Vandiver, Frank E., 1970. *Their Tattered Flags: The Epic of the Confederacy* (New York and Evanston: A Harper's Magazine Press Book).

Weaver, Richard, 1968. *The Southern Tradition at Bay: A History of Post-bellum Thought* (New Rochelle, New York: Arlington House).

Wiley, Bell Irvin, 1968. *The Road to Appomattox* (New York: Atheneum).

Willis, William S., 1963. Divide and Rule: Red, White, and Black in the Southeast. *The Journal of Negro History* 48:157-76.

Woodward, C. Vann, 1951. *Reunion and Reaction: The Compromise of 1877 and the End of Reconstruction* (Boston: Little, Brown and Co.).

Zinn, Howard, 1964. *The Southern Mystique* (New York: Alfred A. Knopf).

The Non-Plantation Southern White in the 17th and 18th Centuries

JOSEPH L. BRENT III

BROADLY, I am here concerned with the conception of difference and the effect of its perception as dangerous. The equating of difference and danger seems to lie at the root of much social enmity. Specifically, I am concerned with how white Europeans, principally lower class Englishmen, reacted to the differences they perceived in the new world. In 1630, that remarkable migration to New England called the Puritan Exodus began. In 1636, Harvard was founded and a year later the Pequot tribe was utterly destroyed. Eleven years before the Exodus, black slaves were introduced into Jamestown and were put to work in the tobacco fields alongside the white contract labor of the time called indentured servants. Eleven years after it, the English philosopher, Thomas Hobbes, published *Leviathan*, his dark prescription for government. Hobbes was born in the year of the Armada, 1588, when as he put it, "my mother bore twins, myself and fear." His remark reflected accurately the temper of the times.

An important part of the transit of culture to North America, often developed differently than I have done here, was the framework of religious beliefs.[1] Of particular interest to me was its dualistic nature in which, especially in popular thought, a cosmic battle between God and Satan was mediated by Christ. The very vocabulary of Christianity exhibited a manichean order presided over by the princes of light and darkness. In the 17th century, the word "black" carried at least these connotations: soiled, dirty, having dark purposes, malignant, deadly, baneful, disastrous, sinister, dismal, gloomy, sad, and threatening. In the same period, "white" carried these, among others: morally or spiritually pure, stainless, spotless, innocent, free from malignity or evil intent (especially as opposed to something characterized as black), propitious, auspicious, and happy. The invisible

for our prest. Security to make Indians & Negro's a checque upon each other least by their Vastly Superior Numbers we should be crushed by one or the other."[39] How did Whites go about this? The essential thing was to make bad blood between them: create suspicion, fear, and hatred. In 1758, James Glen, long governor of South Carolina, explained to William Lyttelton, his inexperienced successor, that "it has been allways the policy of this govert to creat an aversion in them [Indians] to Negroes."[40]

It is difficult to show specifically how Whites went about creating this aversion. Eighteenth century Whites, and especially South Carolinians, were reluctant to write about these things. In 1775, when the American Revolution had already made slaveholders in South Carolina insecure, Colonel Stephen Bull wrote Colonel Henry Laurens about a scheme to create Indian-Negro aversion; but first he dismissed his secretary and wrote this part of his letter in his own hand, admonishing Laurens to keep this scheme secret from all South Carolinians except for a few high officials in the government.[41]

Whites sought to convince Indians that Negroes worked against their best interests. In October, 1715, the Cherokee were on the verge of deserting their Indian confederates in the Yamassee War and joining South Carolina in an attack upon the Creeks. They hoped for a better trade with Charles Town and more security in the South. However, two runaway Negroes from South Carolina came to the Cherokee villages and, according to the South Carolinians, told these Indians a "parcell of lies" which dissuaded the Cherokees from joining the South Carolinians.[42] Later in January, 1716, the Cherokee finally went over to the province; on their part, the South Carolinians agreed to specific commitments for a larger trade at cheap prices and for military support against all enemies of the Cherokee. For a while, it seemed that the province really intended to live up to these commitments and the Cherokee were happy with their new friends in Charles Town.[43] During this time, Whites lost no chance of reminding the Indians that Negroes had almost prevented this boon from coming their way. Negroes were also made out to be dangerous people who would bring hardship and suffering to Indians. In 1739, a small-pox epidemic broke out among the Cherokee and about one thousand warriors died from the disease, and from suicide because of their disfigurement. These Indians despaired so much that they lost confidence in their gods, and the priests destroyed the sacred objects of the tribe. Whites blamed the epidemic on Negroes, telling the Indians that new slaves from Africa had brought the disease to Charles Town.[44] Since this was not the only epidemic that occurred in the

Indian country, we may wonder if Whites had on other accasions also shifted the blame to Negroes.

Whites also contributed to this aversion by using Negro slaves as soldiers against Indians. These slaves were rewarded with goods and sometimes with their freedom. Negroes made good soldiers against other Negroes in rebellion; if they did this against their own people, they certainly had no compunction about fighting Indians.[45] In the Yamassee War, trusted Negroes were drafted and armed and then sent against enemy Indians in the province. Later they were also used against enemy Indians in the interior. When South Carolina invaded the Cherokee country in 1715, Captain Stephen Ford commanded a Negro company. After the Cherokee had come to terms with the province, Ford's company remained in the Cherokee country and took part in attacking the Creeks. In fact, Cherokee chiefs requested this: they said that Negro soldiers would be "very seweasabell [serviceable] to them in Roning after ye Enimy."[46] The French army that invaded the Chickasaw country in 1736 included a company of Negro slaves commanded by a free Negro named Simon; indeed, Simon distinguished himself under fire and was commended by the French.[47] Nevertheless, Whites were reluctant to put muskets in the hands of their slaves; they did not do this until driven by desperation. But in emergencies they were always prepared to do so: legislation was passed in South Carolina in 1747, and renewed from time to time, that authorized the drafting of slaves so long as they did not exceed one third the number of White soldiers.[48] Something besides desperation was behind this: Whites were telling Indians not to count on Negroes in planning another great uprising. This made for Indian antagonism. During the Second Natchez War in 1729, the French accused some Negro slaves of plotting insurrection with the Chouacha Indians, a small harmless tribe living near New Orleans. Although the accusation was unfounded, they armed the Negroes and ordered them to attack this tribe as the sole means of saving their own skins. An on-the-spot reporter tells us that "this expedition rendered the Indians [in Louisiana] mortal enemies of the negroes."[49]

Employing Indians as slave catchers encouraged anti-Negro sentiment among the Indians themselves. Whites paid Indians well for returning fugitive slaves; for instance, at the great Augusta Conference in 1763, the price was set at one musket and three blankets for each slave brought in. The Indian trade was largely based on deerskins, and these skins were sold cheaply to the traders; in order to buy a musket and three blankets, an Indian had to pay about thirty-five skins. This required several months of hunting.[50] Moreover, the hunting grounds were dangerous places; enemies were always lurking about. Hence, an Indian often lost time fighting, if he were lucky enough not to lose his life. In a word, Indians were usually short of goods and in debt. The reward for fugitive slaves was, therefore, something they could rarely afford to turn down. Moreover, the avariciousness of Indians was proverbial in the South.[51] But Indians knew what slavery was like among Whites. They saw its cruelty and brutality whenever they visited the White settlements. They also remembered that Whites had once enslaved Indians in large numbers and occasionally still did so. Indeed, the great fear of Indians was that Whites, and especially South Carolinians, would at sometime make slaves of all Indians in the South. This fear was in the background of all their dealings with Whites.[52] All of this worked in two contradictory ways on Indians. Self-interest made the Indian act as an enemy of Negro freedom; but human feelings made him guilty. Like other men in this ambivalence, he suppressed his guilt with a convenient hostility.

Since it was important that Negroes should fear and hate Indians, it is likely that Whites told their slaves many horror stories about Indians, especially those depicting the terrible things that Indians did to Negroes. Actually it was not difficult to portray Indians in a bad light. Indians did kill and they were cruel. Sometimes their raiding parties striking swiftly and with surprise killed Negroes alongside their White masters.[53] Indians also scalped and otherwise mutilated their victims regardless of race.[54] Besides, Indians were known in the early days to subject their male captives to prolonged and deadly tortures; now and then they did this even in the eighteenth century. In 1730, the French gave the Choctaw three Negroes who had helped the Natchez in 1729. The French expected the Choctaw to torture these Negroes; moreover, they hoped this would discourage Negroes from cooperating with Indians. The French were not disappointed. Father Petit, a Jesuit missionary, reported that these Negroes "have been burned alive with a degree of cruelty which has inspired all the Negroes with a new horror of the Savages, which will have a beneficial effect in securing the safety of the colony."[55] But atrocities were not the main thing. The main thing was that Indians often behaved as real enemies of Negro freedom. To a large extent, Whites encouraged Indians to act this way. As we shall see, this was partly done to make Negroes fear and hate Indians. Given this aim, we assume that Whites publicized these unfriendly acts of Indians among their slaves—and conveniently overlooked their own responsibility. We will now give attention to some situations in which Indians behaved as enemies of Negro freedom.

As we know, Whites employed Indians as slave catchers, and Indians were eager for these jobs. Moreover, Negroes knew that Indians, being expert woodsmen, were better slave catchers than White soldiers and patrols.[56] Negroes also realized that death sometimes awaited the unsuccessful runaway instead of a return to slavery. The Charles Town government executed leaders of fugitive slave parties and those slaves who ran away repeatedly. This government also instructed slave catchers to kill fugitive Negroes when they could not capture them; therefore, dead fugitives were paid for as well as live ones.[57] This encouraged Indians to be more bloodthirsty than White slave catchers: the labor of these fugitives was not going to benefit them. Besides, scalping was more profitable to them than to Whites: Indians could make one scalp look like two or more scalps. To prevent this cheating, the Charles Town government tried to buy only scalps with two ears.[58] Bloodthirstiness was a particular characteristic of Settlement Indians, for slave catching was almost the only opportunity of recapturing the excitement of their old culture. The enthusiasm and violence of Indian slave catchers, as well as the dread Negroes had for them, have been forcibly described by Brickell: "As soon as the Indians have Notice from the *Christians* of their [slaves] being there [in the woods], they disperse them; killing some, others flying for Mercy to the *Christians* . . . rather than fall into the others [Indians] Hands . . . [who] put them to death with the most exquisite Tortures they can invent, whenever they catch them."[59] It is not surprising that a Committee on Indian Affairs in 1727 instructed the Indian Commissioners to have "any Negroe or Negroes Corrected who shall threaten the [Settlement] Indians for Executing any Orders that the said Commissioners shall see fit to give the Indians."[60] Whites did not employ Indians as slave catchers only to recover valuable property and to punish offenders. They also employed them to make their slaves hate Indians. In 1776, some Maroons established themselves on Tybee Island; the Charles Town government secretly arranged for Creek slave catchers to kill these Maroons. Colonel Stephen Bull explained that this would "establish a hatred or aversion between Indians and Negroes."[61]

Indians also permitted and even helped Whites round up Negroes in and about the Indian villages.[62] These Negroes were then conveyed back to slavery. This was a hard blow. These runaways had eluded all the slave catchers and then experienced the intoxication of freedom among the Indians. Some of these runaways only lingered in these villages before moving on to Florida; other runaways settled down in these villages and started making some kind of life for themselves among the Indians. In either case, Indians betrayed them, blasting their hopes. Moreover, these Indians were betraying their own principles of hospitality and sanctuary for strangers—and these principles applied to fugitive Negroes.[63] It seems that Indians, in their greed for trade goods, sometimes betrayed the same fugitives twice. After returning Negroes and collecting their reward, Indians helped these fugitives to escape again before White agents delivered them to their masters. Then these Indians recaptured these fugitives and demanded another full reward from the agents.[64] In time, fugitive Negroes realized that they stayed in jeopardy while among Indians. In 1758, James Beamer, an old Cherokee trader, warned Governor Lyttleton to be discreet in sending for some runaways "for they are always on their Watch and the Least mistrust they have they Will fly Directly to the Woods."[65] In retrieving fugitive slaves from the Indian country, Whites again had the additional motive of making Negroes antagonistic to Indians. Indeed, this motive at times made Whites willingly forego repossessing their slaves. It seems that Whites were pleased when Indians scalped fugitive slaves who lived in Indian villages but would not peaceably surrender. This happened among the Creeks in 1768; Stuart then explained that "this cannot fail of having a very good Effect, by breaking that Intercourse between Negroes & Savages which might have been attended with very troublesome consequences had it continued."[66]

Indians were *bona fide* slave traders. They stole Negroes from White slaveholders in order to sell them to other White slaveholders. Indians had been prepared for this Negro trade by the earlier trade in Indian slaves; for instance, they had learned that male captives were often too valuable to be done away with. Except for raids by Spanish Indians against South Carolina, Indians did not steal too many Negroes in the first half of the eighteenth century. About the only other Indians that regularly raided for Negro slaves were the Chickasaw and other allied tribes of South Carolina living near the Mississippi River. These tribes raided French settlements in Louisiana and French convoys on the Great River. Negroes captured in these raids were sold to Charles Town traders who carried them to South Carolina.[67] This trade did not bring many slaves into the province; the French were always so short of Negroes. For the Negroes, this trade was a calamity. Their capture meant the substitution of one enslavement by a more severe one. Therefore, these Negroes must have been bitter anti-Indian propagandists among the slaves of South Carolina.

After the mid-century, Indians began stealing and selling more and more Negroes. In these years, White settlers increasingly encroached on Indian lands, coming in from almost all sides, and Indians struck back. These years were years of almost continuous warfare between Indians and Whites. Indians made a point of taking Negro slaves from these settlers to discourage their rush into the interior. It was also a fairly easy matter to steal Negroes from slaveholders in transit and in newly established settlements. Moreover, the American Revolution brought a new lawlessness to the South that lasted throughout the century. This meant that more Whites engaged in this Negro trade: these Whites encouraged Indians to steal Negroes and even stole Negroes themselves and disposed of them in the Indian country. British officers during the Revolution had a big part in promoting this Negro stealing: they got Indians, who sided with the British cause, to rob rebel slaveholders. After the Revolution, many White outlaws who were involved in this trade were British sympathizers. In time, this trade became well organized. Negroes were stolen from one part of the Indian frontier and carried into the Indian country and there traded about among Indians, and between Indians and Whites, until they ended up in slavery on another part of the Indian frontier.[68]

Indians had little trouble selling these Negroes. Whites in the frontier settlements never had enough slaves. Moreover, law enforcement was lax. Sometimes Indians sold nearly every Negro they had. In 1784, Alexander McGillivray, the famous half-breed chief, reported that the Creeks were "now pretty well drained of Negroes."[69] This trade extended outside the South. The Cherokee sold Negroes north of the Ohio River and Shawnee traders came from the North into the Creek country to buy Negroes.[70] This trade even extended into the West Indies. In 1783, McGillivray sent Negroes to Pensacola for shipment to Jamaica.[71] It is clear that Indians were avid and heartless slave traders. They looked upon these Negroes as nothing but chattel property. In 1796, John Sevier, Governor of Tennessee and slaveholder, reprimanded the Cherokee for trading Negroes to the Chickasaw for horses: he told them that "you know it is wrong to swop people for horses, for negroes is not horses tho they are black."[72] These were the people Foster and Johnston have made out to be friends of Negroes. We can be sure that eighteenth century Negroes felt differently. We can not say, however, that Whites deliberately fostered this slave trade to create antagonism against Indians. But

we can be sure that Whites did not fail to remind Negroes that
Indians were slave traders.

Finally, Whites employed Indians to help crush slave insurrections.
In the Stono Rebellion of 1739, the most serious insurrection in South
Carolina during the eighteenth century, about eighty Negro slaves
killed more than thirty Whites. At the outset, the Charles Town
government called upon Settlement Indians for help. These Indians
pursued those slaves who eluded the militia at Stono; in a few weeks,
they managed to capture some of these slaves and to kill a few
others.[73] Indians also aided the province in suppressing slave insurrections in 1744 and 1765.[74] Slave insurrections in the eighteenth
century were small-scale affairs; South Carolinians did not need many
Indians to help them restore order in any particular one. What mat-
tered most was speed in putting them down; otherwise, more timid
Negroes might respond to the call of liberty and join the rebel slaves.
Therefore, for this job the Charles Town government turned to
Settlement Indians and Eastern Siouans. Although few in numbers,
these Indians lived closer to White settlements and could be quickly
mustered whenever needed.

The Charles Town government paid Indians high wages for help-
ing suppress slave insurrections. In the Stono Rebellion, each Indian
was given a coat, a flap, a pair of stockings, a hat, a gun, two pounds
of powder, and eight pounds of bullets. The legislature, dominated
by large slaveholders whose eyes were on the future, wanted to increase this payment. It declared that "Indians should be encouraged in
such manner as to induce them always to offer their Service whenever
this Government may have Occasion for them."[75] In 1774, the Natchez,
now living as scattered Settlement Indians in South Carolina after their
defeat by the French in 1729, informed Governor Glen that they
wanted to be "together to be ready to assist the Government in
case of any Insurrection, or Rebellion of the Negroes."[76] We can be
certain that Negroes knew how eager Indians were to help keep them
in slavery.

The Charles Town government did not wait for an uprising
before calling on Indians. This government tried to anticipate trouble
and then prevent it by using Indians to intimidate Negroes. On
November 10, 1739, less than two months after Stono, the legislature ordered its Committee on Indian Affairs to cooperate with its
special committee investigating this insurrection in "finding the most
effectual means for preventing of such Dangers throughout the
province." South Carolinians feared insurrections especially at Christmas, Negroes having so much more free time during these holidays.[77]

During the Christmas of 1716, the Charles Town government ordered Settlement Indians to move nearer White settlements to terrorize the slaves. Moreover, the government made a practice of locating Settlement Indians near places at which slaves might become troublesome. In the summer of 1716, it maintained the Wineau Indians around the Santee settlements "for keeping ye Negroes in awe."[78] But South Carolinians did not rely only on Settlement Indians to prevent insurrections. These tribes and even the Catawba were not large enough to intimidate all Negroes in the province; there were not enough Settlement Indians to station at every danger point. As we know, South Carolinians saw the danger of a big insurrection in every little one. For intimidating all slaves, South Carolina needed at least one big inland tribe. Therefore, the government turned to its most trusted ally and probably the tribe most hostile to Negroes: the Cherokee. In 1737, Lieutenant-Governor Thomas Broughton reported that he was sending for Cherokee warriors "to come down to the settlements to be an awe to the negroes."[79] Thus, a special effort was made after the Yamassee War to keep Negroes isolated from the Cherokee. In 1741, the legislature requested that Broughton purchase two Negro slaves owned by a Cherokee chief so that they could be shipped to the "West Indies or Northern Colonies to prevent any Detriment that they might do this Province by getting acquainted with the Cherokees."[80] It is clear that this intimidation by Indians helped prevent slave insurrections.

CONCLUSIONS

Hostility between Indians and Negroes in the Colonial Southeast was more pronounced than friendliness. Southern Whites were afraid of these two colored races, each of which outnumbered them. Whites were especially afraid that these two exploited races would combine against them. To prevent this combination, Whites deliberately maintained social distance between Indians and Negroes and created antagonism between them. To maintain this social distance, Whites segregated Indians and Negroes from each other. They did this by keeping Indians out of White settlements as much as possible and by trying to keep Negroes out of the Indian country and other out of the way places where these colored races might meet. To create antagonism, Whites deliberately played Indians and Negroes against each other. They pointed out to these races that each was the enemy of the other. To this end of mutual hostility, Whites also used Negroes as soldiers against Indians; on the other hand, they used Indians to catch runaway slaves and to suppress slave insurrections. In the eyes of Negroes, Indians were enemies of Negro freedom. At times, Whites encouraged Indians and Negroes to murder each other. In these ways, Whites created much of the hostility between Indians and Negroes in the eighteenth century.

NOTES

1. Gratitude is extended to Margaret Furcron, Brooklyn College, to Elliott P. Skinner, New York University, and especially to Morton H. Fried, Columbia University, for valuable suggestions, but any infelicities of style or errors of fact are the author's.

2. Laurence Foster, *Negro-Indian Relationships in the Southeast* (Philadelphia, 1935), p. 74; James H. Johnston, "Documentary Evidence of the Relations of Negroes and Indians," *Journal of Negro History*, XIV (January, 1929), 21-23.

3. W. J. Rivers, *A Sketch of the History of South Carolina* (Charleston, 1856), p. 48; W. C. Macleod, *The American Indian Frontier* (New York, 1928), p. 306; Chapman J. Milling, *Red Carolinians* (Chapel Hill, 1940), p. 63.

4. W. L. McDowell (ed.), *Documents relating to Indian Affairs, May 21, 1750-August 7, 1754* (Columbia, 1959), p. 201.

5. *American State Papers, Indian Affairs*, I, 461.

6. John Brickell, *The Natural History of North Carolina* (Dublin, 1737), p. 263.

7. Milling (ed.), *Colonial South Carolina: Two Contemporary Descriptions* (Columbia, 1951), p. 136.

8. David D. Wallace, *South Carolina: A Short History, 1520-1948* (Chapel Hill, 1951), *passim;* Verner W. Crane, *The Southern Frontier, 1670-1732* (Durham, 1928), *passim.*

9. J. H. Easterby (ed.), *Journals of the Commons House of Assembly, September 12, 1739-March 26, 1741* (Columbia, 1952), p. 97.

10. Herbert Aptheker, *American Negro Slave Revolts* (New York, 1943), *passim;* Alexander Garden to Secretary, October 31, 1759, Society for the Propagation of the Gospel in Foreign Parts MSS (later cited as SPG MSS), Series B, II, Pt. 1, 962 Library of Congress; Robert L. Meriwether, *The Expansion of South Carolina, 1729-1765* (Kingsport, 1940), p. 6.

11. Crane, *passim.*

12. Around 1750, Whites were estimated at 30-40,000; Indians, 60,000; Negroes, 70-90,000. Kenneth W. Porter, "Negroes on the Southern Frontier," *Journal of Negro History*, XXXIII (January, 1948), 53-54.

13. Commons House of Assembly to Francis Nicholson, February 3, 1721, Great Britain Public Record Office, Colonial Office (later cited as CO), 5/426, pp. 20-21, Library of Congress.

14. McDowell (ed.), *Journals of the Commissioners of the Indian Trade, September 20, 1710-August 29, 1718* (Columbia, 1955), p. 137.

15. *Colonial Records of North Carolina*, I, 886.

16. Reuben G. Thwaites (ed.), *Jesuit Relations* (Cleveland, 1900), LIX, 189.

17. *Colonial Records of North Carolina*, X, 118.

18. Pepper to Lyttelton, March 30, 1757, South Carolina Indian Book, February 21, 1757-March 6, 1760, p. 19, Library of Congress.

19. Stuart to Gage, November 27, 1767, Thomas Gage Papers, William L. Clements Library, Ann Arbor.

20. Report of Board of Commissioners, August 16, 1779, CO, 5/81, p. 451.

21. Report of Committee on Indian Affairs, May 27, 1742, CO, 5/443, p. 31.

22. McDowell, *Documents*, p. 109.

23. Report of Committee on Indian Affairs, February 29, 1727, CO, 5/430, p. 37.

24. Dunbar Rowland and A. G. Sanders (eds.), *Mississippi Provincial Archives, French Dominion, 1701-1729* (Jackson, 1929), I, 573. Later cited as *MPAFD*.

25. Crane, p. 203; John R. Alden, *John Stuart and the Southern Colonial Frontier, 1754-1775* (Ann Arbor, 1944), pp. 19, 342.

26. Stuart to Gage, March 19, 1765 and December 27, 1767, Gage Papers.

27. Stuart to Gage, September 26, 1767, *ibid*.

28. Report of Committee on Indian Affairs, February 29, 1727, CO, 5/430, p. 37.

29. Stuart to Gage, December 26, 1767, Gage Papers.

30. Taitt to Stuart, September 9, 1773, CO, 5/75, p. 23.

31. *Colonial Records of North Carolina*, III, 131-133; McDowell, *Documents*, p. 190.

32. Pepper, "Some Remarks on the Creek Nation, 1756," William H. Lyttelton Papers, William L. Clements Library.

33. Stuart to Gage, September 26, 1767, Gage Papers.

34. Alden, p. 108; John S. Bassett (ed.), *The Writings of William Byrd* (New York, 1901); pp. 391-392; *Great Britain . . . Calendar of State Papers, Colonial Series, America and the West Indies, 1728-1729* (later cited as *CSP, AWI*), pp. 414-415.

35. Wallace, *The History of South Carolina* (New York, 1934), I, 372.

36. Mark Van Doren (ed.), *The Travels of William Bartram* (New York, 1940), p. 371.

37. Peter Timothy to Lyttelton, November 13, 1759, Lyttelton Papers.

38. E. Merton Coulter (ed.), *The Journal of William Stephens, 1743-1745* (Athens, 1959), II, 245.

39. Ludlam to Secretary, March, 1725, SPG MSS, A, 19, p. 85.

40. Glen to Lyttelton, January 23, 1758, Lyttelton Papers.

41. R. W. Gibbes (ed.), *Documentary History of the American Revolution* (New York, 1855), I, 268-269; "Papers of the Second Council of Safety. . . ," *South Carolina Historical and Genealogical Magazine*, IV (July, 1903), 205-206.

42. Langdon Cheves (ed.), "Journal of the March of the Carolinians into the Cherokee Mountains, 1715-1716," *Year Book of the City of Charleston for 1894*, p. 344.

43. Crane, pp. 180-184, 193-194.

44. Samuel C. Williams (ed.), *Adair's History of the American Indians* (Johnson City, 1928), pp. 244-245.

45. Easterby, p. 64.

46. Crane, p. 183; Cheves, "Journal," p. 348.

47. B. F. French (ed.), *Historical Collections of Louisiana* (New York, 1853), V, 105, 111

48. Wallace, *South Carolina: Short History*, p. 185.

49. *MPAFD*, I, 64; French, pp. 99-101.

50. Stuart to Gage, August 31, 1771, Gage Papers.

51. McDowell, *Documents, passim*.

52. Edmund Atkin to Lyttelton, November 3, 1759, Lyttelton Papers.

53. George Gilmer, *Sketches of Some of the First Settlers of Upper Georgia* (Americus, 1926), p. 251.

54. *American State Papers*, Indian Affairs, I, 452.

55. Thwaites, LXVIII, 197-199.

56. Glen to Newcastle, April 14, 1748, CO, 5/389, p. 58.

57. Aptheker, "Maroons within the Present Limits of the United States," *Journal of Negro History*, XXIV (April 1939), 169.

58. Samuel Hazard (ed.), *Pennsylvania Archives, 1756-1760* (Philadelphia, 1853), III, 200; Easterby, p. 681.

59. Brickell, p. 273.

60. Report of Committee on Indian Affairs, February 29, 1727, CO, 5/430, p. 37.

61. Gibbes, p. 268-269; "Papers of the Second Council of Safety," pp. 205-206.

62. Stuart to Gage, December 26, 1767, Gage Papers.

63. Francis Baily, *Journal of a Tour in Unsettled Parts of North America in 1796 and 1797* (London, 1856), pp. 370-371.

64. Taitt to Stuart, July 13, 1777, CO, 5/79, p. 25.

65. Beamer to Lyttelton, May 20, 1758, Lyttelton Papers.

66. Stuart to Gage, July 2, 1768, Gage Papers.

67. *MPAFD*, III, 635.

68. Joseph B. Lockey (ed.), *East Florida, 1783-1785* (Berkeley, 1949), *passim;* John W. Caughey (ed.), *McGillivray of the Creeks* (Norman, 1938), *passim.*

69. *Ibid.,* p. 67.

70. "An Indian Talk," *American Historical Magazine, III* (January, 1898), 85; Adelaide L. Fries (ed.), *The Records of the Moravians in North Carolina* (Raleigh, 1941), V, 1985.

71. D. C. Corbitt (ed.), "Papers Relating to the Georgia-Florida Frontier, 1784-1800," *Georgia Historical Quarterly,* XXI (March, 1937), 75.

72. Williams (ed.), "Executive Journal of General John Sevier," *East Tennessee Historical Society's Publications,* I, (1929), 119.

73. Easterby, *passim.*

74. Milling, *Red Carolinians,* p. 229; Wallace, *South Carolina: Short History,* p. 185.

75. Easterby, pp. 65, 76-77.

76. South Carolina Council Journal, December 11, 1743-December 8, 1744, CO, 5/448, pp. 187-188.

77. Easterby, pp. 24, 69.

78. Wallace, *History of South Carolina,* I, 185; McDowell, *Journals,* p. 80.

79. Quoted in Wallace, *History of South Carolina,* I, 368.

80. Easterby (ed.), *Journals of the Commons House of Assembly, May 18, 1741-July 10, 1742* (Columbia, 1953), p. 45.

The Indian in the Old South

John H. Peterson, Jr.

FAR too many studies of historic Southern Indians have erroneously assumed that they were socio-cultural isolates, existing outside a complex, stratified society that included several kinds of white and black people. It is my intention to show that this erroneous assumption has resulted from a failure to attempt to deal with the totality of human social relations in the Southeast as they changed through time.[1] Without some framework capable of including all major socio-cultural elements it is impossible to adequately describe or understand the position of the Indian in the Old South. I will suggest a conceptual framework which will permit the analysis of the total social relations in the Southeast through time and as a test case indicate how it is able to account for the historical experience of a single Southern Indian group, the Choctaws.

The description of the Southern Indian as a social isolate stems in large measure from the limitations associated with the term "Old South," which came into usage following Henry W. Grady's coinage of the term "New South" to indicate and emphasize the growing importance of manufacturing in the South in the 1880s. In opposition to this, the term "Old South" came to designate the earlier historical period in the southeastern United States.

Historians have debated the utility of the term "Old South" and its implication of discrete historical periods as opposed to a recognition of continuity and the evolutionary nature of change in Southern society (Cotterill 1964). This argument for continuity may have validity as it pertains to white Southerners, but there is no question of the drastic and sudden changes in the social position of non-whites, especially Indians, in Southern society.

A brief examination of historical titles dealing with the Old South indicates that this period is most frequently considered to begin with European settlement in the southeastern United States and to end with the Civil War or Reconstruction, and that the geographic area covered under the term "Old South" only included territory under English or American control or occupation.[2] Indeed, the areas of the present southeastern United States which were not part of the Old South are often identified by the term "Old Southwest." The westward movement of the frontier thus represents the expansion of the Old South into the Old Southwest. The term "Old Southwest" is sometimes thought to be limited to that portion of the Southeast west of the original seaboard colonies. However, Henderson's (1920) title, *The Conquest of the Old Southwest: The Romantic Story of the Early Pioneers into Virginia, The Carolinas, Tennessee and Kentucky, 1740-1790,* clearly indicates that the Old Southwest began at the borders of the Old South.

In other words, the term "Old South" designates a recognizable period in the history of English-speaking immigrants and their descendants in southeastern North America beginning with settlement and lasting until the Civil War or shortly thereafter. As a historical period, the Old South has meaning only in terms of the activities and way of life of these immigrants and the society they established. It does not pertain to, in fact it excludes Southern Indians, their way of life, and their history. Historical scholarship on Negro life in the Old South has increased in recent years, but this literature is yet so small and information on non-whites in more general histories so slight that one is still justified in saying that the history of the Old South remains to this day a primarily white history.

The degree to which Southern Indians are excluded from histories of the Old South can be further demonstrated by examining histories and historiographical writing for information about Southern Indians. In many works one looks in vain for any mention of Indians (Dodd 1937; Hart 1910; Simkins 1948; Eaton 1949; Stephenson 1959). This may at times be justified in terms of the particular interest of an author, but it is hardly excusable in general works on the Old South where the geography is more often described than are the Indians. Where mention is made of the Southern Indians, it is often sandwiched between descriptions of geography and colonial settlement. Two examples of this approach are Cotterill's (1939) chapter on "The Oldest Inhabitants" and Betterworth's (1964) chapter on "The First Mississippians." Furthermore, the few accounts that do exist more nearly resemble static, ahistorical descriptions of the natural landscape than descriptions of historical events in the lives of human beings. The historians can scarcely be blamed for such static descriptions, since most of their material both summarizes and follows the form of standard ethnographic accounts by anthropologists. As a result, the Southern Indian in history has become like a part of the natural landscape, serving primarily as a setting for the territorial expansion and development of the Old South.

In many scholarly works there is one further subject or section that is often included before the history of the Old South can really begin, and this is a description of colonial rivalries and the struggle between France, Spain, and England for control of the Old Southwest. With the gradual demise of competing colonial powers, the emergence of the United States as a nation, and the final elimination of the Indians, the Old Southwest vanishes and the history of the Old South begins. In fact, some studies do not recognize the emergence of the South as a recognizable region until around 1820, after most of these events had occurred (Rankin 1965:3).

As a result, in most Southern histories the Indian is merely a kind of prologue, and the main portion of the history of the Old South begins only after his removal or destruction. Admittedly, Indians continued to occupy most of the Old Southwest after white settlements covered most of Virginia, North and South Carolina, and eastern Georgia, but in such cases would it be correct to say that the Indian inhabitants of the Old Southwest were part of the Old South? They were not within the geographic confines of the continuous territory occupied by English speaking settlers of European ancestry, nor were they for much of the period within the control of the government of these settlers. Certainly they were influenced by European contact, and one can talk about the relations between Indians and the inhabitants of the Old South, or one can describe scattered tribal remnants within the contiguous territory occupied by the holders of Old Southern culture. But the masses of Southern Indians could never be considered to be in the Old South. Only after the final massive Indian removal in the 1830s could the term "Old South" be applied to all the states in the Southeast.

Here we can see at least part of the reason for the false assumption that the Indians were a relatively isolated socio-cultural element existing outside a complex, stratified society known as the South. The problem lies not so much with the definition of "Indian," as it does with the use of the term "Old South" to identify primarily the post-settlement pre-Reconstruction period of the history of English-speaking people of European ancestry living in the Southeastern United States. The Indian was not thought to be part of the Old South simply because of the continuing description of the Old South as a society dominated by whites and composed exclusively of whites and Negroes.

The study of the Southern Indian as a social isolate can not be blamed entirely on historical research on the South. Students of Indian history have also failed to see a unified picture of the Southeast. Indian historians, like students of the Old South, frequently begin their books with a description of the Southern Indian in terms of "traditional culture" with detailed references to ethnographic works. They then generally proceed to write the history of a particular tribe. Where the study is of one of the five civilized tribes, the study usually follows the removal of the mass of tribal members to Oklahoma and continues their history there while ignoring the Indians who remained in the South (Debo 1934; McReynolds 1957; Woodward 1963). The students of Indian history are likely to describe in detail the relations of the Indians with non-Indians, and in fact the political relations between the Indians and the non-Indians constitute a large measure of their study. However, with their central focus on the Indian people, they do not describe the Indian *in* the Old South, and their relevant historical periods are not the same as those of the Southern historian with his interest in European immigrant society.

Like the students of the Old South, the beginning point for the Indian historian is initial white contact, but the removal west constitutes the basic end of a historical period for the Indian historian. The second period deals with the establishment of tribal government in Oklahoma. While the Indians in Oklahoma were significantly affected by the Civil War, this event was far less significant than the beginning of Oklahoma statehood and the ending of the Indian "nations." Since the recognized Indian nations were never an integral part of the Old South, the writers of these Indian histories largely ignore the Old South. Dealing with different people and recognizing different historical periods, the Indian historian has little or nothing to contribute to discussions about the Old South.

Not all historians of the Southern Indians have followed the subjects of their studies to Oklahoma. Some have dealt with groups who were never removed (Brown 1966), and others have dealt with those who were left behind (Bounds 1964). But in either case, the historian tends to place major emphasis on the period before the removal or destruction of the majority of the Indian group. Removal or destruction is the key turning point in the history of the individual Indian group, and by comparison the history of the remaining period is extremely brief and rarely deals in depth with the relations with non-Indians.

Finally, turning from the historian dealing with the Old South or with Indian history to the ethnographer focusing on the Indians themselves, we find preoccupation with a "traditional culture." The unfortunate consequence of this attention given to traditional culture and to survivals of traditional practices is that little attention is given to the history or events between the original documentary descriptions of the people and the ethnographer's later personal observations and research. Where the ethnographer has been primarily interested in the contemporary Indians rather than traditional culture, he has concentrated on various points of theoretical interest, such as acculturation, thereby substituting measurable social phenomena for chronological history.

At this point it should be clear that the position of the Indian in the Old South can be discussed only by changing the generally established meaning of the term Old South, or perhaps better by rejecting the term altogether as primarily applying to only one ethnic group. The studies of Indians by Indian historians and ethnographers offer us no satisfactory alternatives. Indian historians, like the Southern historians, use a point of view suitable to only one ethnic group, and ethnographers are too often prone to ignore history altogether or to focus on short historical periods.

I am therefore suggesting that the only way to avoid dealing with the Indian as a social isolate is to avoid following any one of these scholarly traditions, trying instead to merge or combine their approaches and strengths. This requires that we set as our goal the description of the position of the Indian in the totality of human social relations in southeastern North America from the time of white settlement to reconstruction. In order to do this, I will suggest a framework for describing the totality of human social relations in the Southeast between these two events and the position of the Indian in this totality.

Any statement of the position of the Indian in the Southeast in relation to non-Indians must incorporate a historical framework that is meaningful to both Indian and non-Indian experience. By combining the historical periods of the Southern and Indian historians, we find two established historical periods during the time span under consideration. As we have seen, a historical period that seems to have meaning for English-speaking European immigrants in the Southeast is the period from initial settlement to Reconstruction. For the Southern Indian, this same period seems better conceived as *two* historical periods, the first lasting from white settlement to the removal or destruction of the Indian group and the second being the history of those remaining behind after the mass removals or destruction. A combination of the two historical experiences of both groups involves a recognition that the period between white settlement and reconstruction comprises two historical periods divided by Indian removal or destruction.

This additional distinction is required only if we are interested in the relation of Indians to other inhabitants of the Southeast. Thus, the combined framework indicates changes in the total social relations of inhabitants of the Southeast, and not just changes within one group.

Given the three major turning points listed above, four major periods or phases can be identified in terms of the total human social relations in the Southeast. These periods, particularly the earlier ones, can be more correctly called phases since the key events took place only gradually, with large sections of the Southeast remaining unaffected by the changes for some time. These phases are:

Phase	*Event ending phase*
Traditional	White settlement
International	Destruction or removal of Indian groups
Slavery	Civil War and Reconstruction
Post-slavery	Civil rights movement

Prior to European discovery and settlement, social relations among the inhabitants of the Southeast were limited to traditional relations among Indian groups. Details of social relations existing among the different Indian groups at the time of white contact are far from completely understood and indeed probably will never be completely understood, although archaeological and ethnohistorical research is making some headway. White exploration and settlement introduced a new complex of ideas about inter-group relations based on Western European ideas about relations among nations. While traditional relations long continued to be the pattern among Indian groups remote from white settlement, the expansion of white settlement and the emerging competition between colonial powers gradually made the entire Southeast a battleground between Britain, France, and Spain. Each colonial power attempted to secure additional lands or favors from Indian groups adjacent to them. These Indian groups were most often accorded legal recognition as Indian "nations," equal or semi-equal allies of the particular colonial power. Their leaders were given European titles and often commissions within the military hierarchy of the colonial power. Gradually almost all Indian groups were brought into the spheres of influence of competing colonial powers.

The very concept of Indian "nation" seems related to this colonial rivalry. Possession of lands and a large number of warriors were the defining characteristic of an Indian nation for the colony of South Carolina in the eighteenth century (Hudson 1970:47). Loss of fighting men or land ended the existence of the nation. Even the Indian nations which continued to hold land and which had a considerable population were doomed when the period of colonial rivalry came to an end. With the rise of the new American nation and the defeat of its Colonial rivals, international relations in the Southeast came to an end. There was no longer any utility in the United States as a sovereign state recognizing individual Indian nations, nor were there international allies to whom the Indian nations could turn for assistance. Southern state governments were able to unilaterally terminate Indian sovereignty and force the Federal Government to adopt a removal policy. During the 1830s the bulk of Indians remaining in the Southeast were removed to Oklahoma, often with their tribal governments intact. This, however, was not the end of Indians in the Southeast, contrary to the impressions one would receive from the literature. Many small groups of Indians remained behind where they became what might be called an ethnic group within a single pluralistic society, rather than a nationality within an international society.

Even before the end of the international period in the Old South, whites and blacks were masters and slaves. It is certainly true that the mass of whites were never slave-owners, but most aspired to this position, especially in the newly opened Indian frontier lands, and it is equally true that almost all Negroes were slaves. The end of the international period had little effect on the relations between whites and Negroes within the Old South, but if our framework for analysis of social relations within the Southeast is to include all peoples, we must recognize that for the Indian the position of being a third ethnic group in a society based on rather clear-cut and mutually exclusive social relations between white and black was most difficult. The remaining Indians were not land-owners, as were most whites, nor were they slaves, as were most blacks. They were the people in between, belonging to neither of the two largest social groups in the Old South. As such, they had little choice but to retreat onto inaccessible or undesirable land where as squatters they maintained to some degree their traditional life, isolated from both whites and blacks.

This state of affairs continued for the end of the international period until the end of the slave period. Following the Civil War and

Reconstruction, Negro slaves were freed, and several variants of the share-cropping system arose to replace slavery. In the changing economic situation, even some whites became sharecroppers, and the idea of working on shares was not restricted to a single ethnic group, as was slave status. The basic change in agricultural work made it possible for Indians to begin to work as sharecroppers without accepting the slave status or demanding the status of free white landowners, which would have been necessary under the plantation system.

This, then, summarizes the basic framework for viewing Indian participation in the Old South. To glance forward a moment, one can observe that both Negroes and Indians emerged only gradually from sharecropping and marginal agricultural labor and began attempting to be true equals with whites, first in industrial jobs and more recently in politics and education. The impact of the Civil Rights movement in the South often benefitted Indians as much as Negroes. The growing consciousness of a separate identity as Southern Indians, the increasing power of tribal governments, and the formation of a United Southeastern Tribes all could be interpreted as signaling a fourth stage in Southern Indian history. To cite only one example, in 1968 the Mississippi Choctaws regained the right to administer justice to their own people on their own land, and a tribal court began operating for the first time in almost one hundred and forty years (Dean 1970).

Having presented a framework for analysis of the position of the Indian in the total social relations of the inhabitants of the Southeast, our final task will be to see how this framework throws light on the history of a particular tribe, the Mississippi Choctaws. The available literature on the Choctaws demonstrates the traditional historical approach to the Southern Indians discussed above. Traditional Choctaw culture and more recent survivals have been described by Swanton (1931). The best history of the Choctaw people virtually ignores the continued presence of Choctaws in Mississippi after removal, instead focusing on the Choctaw people in Oklahoma (Debo 1934). The most widely read general history of the state of Mississippi (Bettersworth 1964) has a chapter on the traditional Indian culture but virtually ignores the presence of Choctaws in Mississippi after removal. The only published work on the history of the Mississippi Choctaws (Bounds 1964) devotes 50 pages to traditional culture and early history but only 3 pages to history between removal and the establishment of the Choctaw Agency in 1918. In other words, the prevailing trends in studies of Southern Indians and Southern society has resulted in an almost total blank in the history of the Choctaws from the time of removal until relatively recent years.

In reading standard accounts, one gains the impression that there was little change in the condition of the Choctaws in Mississippi from the time of removal until recently. In the words of one author (Bounds 1964:51), "They were marking time in a 'no man's land'." My own research (Peterson 1970) has led me to the opposite conclusion. Far from marking time, a radical change in the position of the Choctaws in the local society occurred between the time of removal and the present day, and this change seems to have been part of a more general restructuring of human social relations throughout the Southeast. Moreover, this was only one of a series of such changes experienced by the Choctaws in social relations with other peoples. This can be seen by examining the Choctaws in the different phases of Southern Indian history that were identified above.

Although "traditional" Choctaw social and ceremonial life has been described in detail by Swanton, much of this information comes after the period of colonial rivalries was well established. We know virtually nothing about the relations between the Choctaws and their nearest neighbors, such as the Natchez to the West and the Chickasaw to the North, before the relations among these groups became dictated to a large degree by colonial rivalries. Moreover, the early maps of the area show numerous small "tribes" whose relationships with the Natchez, Chickasaw, and Choctaw remain unknown. In short, we are not even sure who was or was not a Choctaw, much less the relations between Choctaws and other groups before the Choctaws were identified as a nation by Europeans and began to be influenced by colonial rivalries. Colonial military operations and the inter-Indian warfare promoted by colonial powers quickly reduced the number of identifiable Indian nations in Mississippi to the Chickasaw, who allied with the English, and the Choctaw, who were allied with the French.

During this period of international rivalry the Choctaws rapidly adopted many of the traits of European settlers. In this regard they were exceeded in the Southeast only by the Cherokees. But the declining cultural differences between some members of the Choctaw "nation" and members of the American nation did not change the fact that to a large extent the Choctaws continued to control internal affairs within their borders, although they came increasingly under the political control of the United States.

The international period ended for the Choctaws when state jurisdiction was unilaterally extended over them, making it illegal for their tribal government to function and granting all Choctaws the status of Mississippi citizens, thereby making them subject to all state laws. The Choctaws were now *in* the Old South for the first time. The response of many of the Choctaws was to accept the necessity of removal to Oklahoma where they were told their existence as a nation would not be challenged.

Large numbers of Choctaws, however, initially preferred to accept their changed status and remain in their traditional homeland as citizens of the state of Mississippi, an option open to them under the terms of the removal treaty. The experiences of this group support the proposition that with the ending of their status as an Indian nation there was drastic change in the position of Indians in the Southeast. While slavery had existed in the Choctaw "nation," it had little effect on the majority of Choctaws; it was only with the extension of state laws over the Choctaws that social relations based on slavery had a major impact on the relations of Choctaws with non-Choctaws. The Choctaws remaining in Mississippi rapidly lost possession of their land. As a result, they were left free but landless in an agricultural society in which one social group was primarily composed of white landowners and a second social group was primarily composed of non-landowning Negro slaves.

Although the Choctaws, like other Southeastern Indians, had been forced into slavery during earlier times, the use of Indian slaves had largely died out by the late eighteenth century as the supply of Negro slaves increased and as slave owners found their working abilities to be more satisfactory (Lauber 1913). Whites who could afford to use extra agricultural labor bought Negro slaves. Poor white landowners could exchange agricultural labor with each other, but the only alternative to this was the use of slave labor; there was no generally established pattern of wage agricultural work. But even if whites had offered to use Choctaws in agricultural work, Choctaws could not have accepted such work without becoming slaves in their own eyes (Rouquette n.d.: 12-14).

As a result, there was no social role in agriculture in the Old South for a free, non-white, non-landowning Indian. The only solution for the Choctaws was to become squatters on marginal agricultural land, isolated from both Negroes and whites. The existence of large numbers of Indian and mixed-blood Indian populations along the eastern seaboard and the Southern Appalachians in isolated areas with marginal soil indicates that the Choctaw experience was far from unique and that this was probably the only manner in which the Indian could continue to exist in a society based on slavery. I would suggest that a detailed examination of the origin of isolated Indian settlements throughout the Southeast would indicate that many of them are the result of Indians remaining after the passing of the line of white settlements. Also one would expect that a study of "settlement" Indians in the colonial South (Hudson 1970:56) would demonstrate that they faced a problem similar to that of the Choctaws after 1830.

It seems probable that the Choctaws remaining in Mississippi after the period of Indian removal were more isolated from contact with whites than they had been prior to removal. The tribal government had allowed whites to move freely within Choctaw borders, and traders, government agents, and missionaries had sought them out. It was this intensive interaction within the borders of the Choctaw "nation" that resulted in the rapid rate of adoption of European practices. After they became citizens, however, the remaining Choctaws were a disinherited ethnic group rather than an influential "nation." Within Choctaw borders prior to removal a white man could aspire to be equal to a Choctaw. But within the borders of the Old South it was almost impossible for a Choctaw to aspire to be the equal of a white man. Yet there were those few who did, such as Greenwood LaFlore, the wealthy educated half-blood who prior to removal was one of the leaders of the Choctaw nation. He was influential in securing the execution of the removal treaty and was generously rewarded by the Federal Government with a gift of land in the Mississippi Delta. Here he became a wealthy and respected plantation owner and was elected to the Mississippi legislature. It is doubtful if a full-blood could have accomplished the same even if he had owned property and slaves. Certainly the equally prominent leader Moshulatubbee, a full-blood, was unable to do so. Thus, the wealthy land- and slave-owning half-breed could be accepted in white society in Mississippi after the removal of the Choctaw "nation." Other Choctaws had the choice of remaining in Mississippi as isolated squatters, following traditional subsistence agricultural practices, or of leaving for Oklahoma. In either case, they were separated from both Southern whites and Negroes.

The contention that the position of the Indians who remained after removal was determined in large part by the established social relationship between black and white under the plantation system can be verified in two ways. The change in the position of the Indians following the loss of their status as a "nation" has already been described. A second test can be provided by looking forward to the end of the plantation period and ascertaining the change in the position of the Choctaws following the change in black-white relations brought by the Civil War and Reconstruction.

So far as can be determined, the Choctaws seem to have retreated deeper into the swamplands in the sand-clay hills of Mississippi during the Civil War and the more localized violence of Reconstruction. Thus, while major changes in relations between Negroes and whites occurred, there is no evidence that any change occurred in the position of Indians as isolated squatters. However, in the late 1870s, violence began to taper off as local whites re-established their control over politics and government. By this time, the sharecropping system had been well established. Negroes had developed their own associations of Negro churches and through these a system of Negro schools (Wharton 1965). Significantly, only after these developments had proven successful do we find evidence of the Choctaws moving out of their rural isolation and entering the agricultural system as sharecroppers.

While the exact date of Choctaw entrance into sharecropping is not known, church records indicate that the first Christian church among the Choctaws was established only a short time after the establishment of a Negro church near one of the Choctaw communities. From this base, Choctaw churches spread to other Choctaw communities largely through the Choctaws' own efforts. And like the Negro churches, the Choctaw churches became centers for the first Indian schools since removal. This occurred on an informal basis even before the state of Mississippi finally established a school system for Choctaw children in 1890.

While it is always difficult to prove historical causality, especially in dealing with the poorly documented history of Indians in the Southeast between removal and more recent times, in the Choctaw case the rapidity of change seems to speak for itself. From the 1830s until the 1870s there was little change among the Mississippi Choctaws. All available information seems to indicate that by any standard the Choctaws in Mississippi in 1875 were on the whole less acculturated than the Choctaws in Mississippi in 1830. During this forty-five year period literacy had almost if not completely vanished, and most remaining Choctaws were non-Christians. In 1879, there was recorded the first conversion of a Mississippi Choctaw to Christianity to take place since removal. Within fifteen years churches were established in most major Choctaw communities where their services successfully competed with traditional ball games and dances. During the same period, the majority of Indian children in communities with Indian churches were enrolled in school. Although the Mississippi Choctaws received some financial help from the state government and from missionary societies, this development depended to an impressive degree on Choctaw initiative. One can only conclude that the changes in social relations between Negroes and whites that made possible certain developments among Negro Mississippians made similar developments possible among Choctaw Mississippians. The rapid transformation of the Choctaw communities is so dramatic that I have elsewhere referred to it as the development of the New Choctaw communities (Peterson 1970).

The wider point involved, however, is the need for understanding the total human social relations in a complex society if one is to adequately deal with any one group. At least five theses and dissertations (Beckett 1949; Deweese 1957; Farr 1948; Tolbert 1958; Langford 1953) cover Choctaw history during this critical period, and their authors exhibit ample knowledge of the facts mentioned above. However, the revolutionary change involved escapes them as does the relationship between change in Choctaw relations with non-Choctaws and changes in black and white relations. These scholars failed in this respect not because they did not know the Choctaw data, but rather because they attempted to interpret it without understanding the full range of human social relations in a complex society.

If the framework I have suggested for analysis of Southern Indian history is correct, then the same type of change that has just been described for the Choctaws should be indicated in other works dealing with Southern Indians during this period. Hudson (1970) provides ample confirmation that the Catawbas were undergoing a similar experience. Unlike the Choctaw, the Catawbas have had a small state reservation since colonial times, but it was inadequate to provide a livelihood for all the people. Following the establishment of the sharecropping system, Catawbas began for the first time to leave the reservation for a year or two to sharecrop and then return. Hudson indicates that the changed social relations between white, black, and mestizo resulted in the Catawba undergoing an "identity crisis" at this time. Although some of them had previously attended white churches, the Catawbas became converts to Mormonism after being contacted by a missionary in 1883, only four years after the first modern conversion of a Mississippi Choctaw. The establishment of a Catawba Indian church was related to the Catawbas' building their own school in 1897, approximately twelve years after the Choctaws established their first school in a Choctaw church.

Although information is scattered, the role of the church seems especially indicative of the changed position of all the Southern Indians after Reconstruction. Lindquist's (1923) report on a survey of Protestant mission activities to Indians in 1921 indicates that several other Southern Indian groups were becoming more active Christians in this same time period, some of them for the first time. The following table summarizes information from Lindquist plus the previously mentioned Choctaw and Catawba information.

POST-RECONSTRUCTION RELIGIOUS DEVELOPMENTS AMONG SOUTHERN INDIANS

Indian Group	Date	Religious Activity Initiated	Previous Activity
Choctaw	1879	Self-initiated Baptist	
	1883	Catholic Mission	None
Cherokee	1880	Methodist Mission	Baptist churches(?)
Alabama (Texas)	1881	Presbyterian Mission	?
Catawba	1883	Mormon Mission	Scattered activity
Seminole	1891	National Indian Assn. Mission	None
"Qua-she-tee" (Louisiana)	1896	Congregationalist Mission	?

Perhaps this is sufficient to suggest that just as there was a rapid development of separate churches for Negroes after the Civil War, so there was a rapid development of separate churches for Indians in the Southeast at this time also. This plus the Choctaw data mentioned above suggests that it would be profitable to look for major changes in all aspects of life of Southern Indians as well as of mixed-blood groups in the Southeast following Reconstruction with its changes in black and white relationships.

In conclusion, I have argued that it is impossible to adequately describe the position of the Indian in the Old South without some conceptual framework capable of dealing with the totality of human social relations in the Southeast as they changed through time. Three research traditions—southern history, Indian history, and ethnography—deal to some extent with the Southern Indian. The erroneous assumption that Southern Indians were socio-cultural isolates stems

in large part from the isolated and specific interests of these three
fields of study. The history of the Old South is written primarily in
terms of the experience of English-speaking European settlers and
their descendants in the Southeast. History written exclusively from
this frame of reference ignores non-European inhabitants of the
Southeast except as they directly affected the white Southerner and
his society. Indian history and ethnography provide no satisfactory
alternatives. Indian history is concerned primarily with the historical
experience of the Indian nations and ignores Indians remaining in
the Southeast after Indian removals. Anthropologists have focused
primarily on the traditional culture or contemporary life of the
Southern Indians, largely ignoring their history.

The lack of Indian history, especially history in relation to other
socio-cultural elements in the Southeast can be avoided by uniting
the approaches of the Southern historian, the Indian historian, and
the social scientist and constructing a conceptual framework capable
of dealing with the totality of social relations in the Southeast as
they changed through time. This paper has suggested a conceptual
framework consisting of four major historical periods or phases. The
first or traditional phase consisted of the time when social relations in
the Southeast were limited to those of the Indian people. This phase
was gradually merged into a second or international phase following
white settlement when Indian groups became identified as nations in
the Western European sense and became involved in a system of
competing colonial alliances. During this phase, the Southern Indians
increasingly adopted European patterns of life, but with the end of
colonial rivalry in the Southeast, all Indian nations had been destroyed
or were shortly to be removed as nations to Oklahoma. Following
removal or destruction of the majority of Indian people, the remaining
Southern Indians entered a third phase of their history. During this
phase, they became an isolated and ignored ethnic group because
they had no place in the rigid structure of Southern society based
on non-white slaves and free whites. Only with the breakdown of
this social system and the ending of the slave phase was it possible
for the isolated Indian groups to begin to have greater interaction
with non-Indian groups. The distinctions between these four phases
are not of equal importance in dealing with all social groups within
the Southeast, but all phases are necessary for understanding the
changes in the social position of the Southern Indian in the totality
of social relations in the Southeastern United States.

The utility of this conceptual framework was examined in terms
of the history of the Choctaw Indians of Mississippi. Choctaw history

confirmed the adequacy of the proposed framework, and, more important, indicated that the framework focused attention on important aspects of the Choctaw experience that had been ignored by research using alternative approaches. Although fragmentary, information on other Southern Indians indicates that their histories paralleled that of the Choctaws. This would suggest that fuller confirmation of the conceptual framework herein presented can be found in comparative research on the largely neglected post-removal history of the Southern Indians.

The importance of the conceptual frameworks representing the diverse historical experiences of separate ethnic or social groups in a complex society reaches beyond the subject of this paper. If the comparative research suggested above validates the conceptual framework suggested here, it will have demonstrated the necessity of a holistic approach to the historical study of complex societies. Otherwise, both descriptions and histories of individual social groups tend to be based on situations and events which have meaning primarily to one group. As a result we have a limited and biased understanding of total social relations as they have changed through time, and our history as it is written cannot avoid being ethnocentric.

NOTES

1. I am indebted to several individuals for the ideas expressed in this paper. Charles Hudson stimulated my interest in the problems of plural societies and their history as they applied to the Southern United States. His research on the Catawba (1970) was especially influential in establishing the difference between Indian "nations" and "settlement" Indians in the colonial South. J. C. Vinson and Joseph Parks instructed me in historical methodology and together with Hudson encouraged the questioning of both established facts and assumptions. Emmett York, Chairman of the Choctaw Tribal Council, patiently helped me to understand that a Southern Indian's view of Southern history is quite different from that of a Southern white. Finally, it was only through a reading of Southern Negro history, especially from Vernon Wharton (1965), that the full significance of post-removal Choctaw history began to occur to me. Although I am indebted to these men for the originality of their ideas, responsibility for the use or distortion of these ideas is truly mine.

2. A detailed examination of all the literature on the Old South is beyond the scope of this paper. Southern historiography is considered in detail in Link and Patrick (1965). Recent trends in Southern historical writing are described by Stephenson (1964). A sample of the interests of Southern historians can be seen in the collection of almost thirty years of presidential addresses of the Southern Historical Association edited by Tindall (1964). In addition, specific histories bearing the title Old South or including it as a major subsection include: Cotterill (1939); Dodd (1937); Eaton (1949, 1961); Phillips (1941); and Simkins (1948, 1967).

132 *Red, White, and Black*

REFERENCES

Beckett, Charlie M., 1949. Choctaw Indians in Mississippi Since 1830. Unpublished M.A. thesis, Oklahoma A. and M.

Bettersworth, John K., 1964. *Mississippi Yesterday and Today* (Austin: Steck-Vaughn Co.).

Bounds, Thelma V., 1964. *Children of Nanih Waiya* (San Antonio: Naylor Co.).

Brown, Douglas Summers, 1966. *The Catawba Indians: The People of the River* (Columbia: University of South Carolina Press).

Cotterill, Robert S., 1939. *The Old South* (Glendale: The Arthur H. Clark Co.).

----------------------------------, 1964. The Old South to the New. In *The Pursuit of Southern History: Presidential Addresses of the Southern Historical Association 1935-1963*, George Brown Tindall, ed. (Baton Rouge: Louisiana State University Press).

Dean, S. B., 1970. Law and Order Among the First Mississippians. Mimeographed Report, Association on American Indian Affairs, Inc., Washington, D. C.

Debo, Angie, 1934. *The Rise and Fall of the Choctaw Republic* (Norman: University of Oklahoma Press).

Deweese, Orval H., 1957. The Mississippi Choctaws. Unpublished M.A. thesis, Mississippi State University.

Dodd, William E., 1937. *The Old South Struggles for Democracy* (New York: Macmillan Co.).

Eaton, Clement, 1949. *A History of the Old South* (New York: Macmillan Co.).

---------------------------------- , 1961. *The Growth of Southern Civilization 1790-1860* (New York: Harper Bros.).

Farr, Eugene, 1948. Religious Assimilation: A Case Study of the Adoption of Christianity by the Choctaw Indians of Mississippi. Unpublished Ph.D. diss., New Orleans Baptist Theological Seminary.

Hart, Albert B., 1910. *The Southern South* (New York: D. Appleton and Co.).

Henderson, 1920. *The Conquest of the Old Southwest: The Romantic Story of the Early Pioneers into Virginia, the Carolinas, Tennessee and Kentucky, 1740-1790* (New York: Century Co.).

Hudson, Charles M., 1970. *The Catawba Nation* (Athens: University of Georgia Press).

Langford, Etha Myerl, 1953. A Study of the Educational Development of the Choctaw Indians of Mississippi. Unpublished M.A. thesis, Mississippi Southern College.

Lauber, Almon Wheeler, 1913. *Indian Slavery in Colonial Times Within the Present Limits of the United States* (New York: Longmans, Green and Co.).

Lindquist, G. E. E., 1923. *The Red Man in the United States* (New York: George H. Doran Co.).

Link, Arthur S. and Rembert W. Patrick, eds., 1965. *Writing Southern History: Essays in Historiography in Honor of Fletcher M. Green* (Baton Rouge: Louisiana State University).

McReynolds, Edwin C., 1957. *The Seminoles* (Norman: University of Oklahoma Press).

Peterson, John H. Jr., 1970. The Mississippi Band of Choctaw Indians: Their Recent History and Current Social Relations. Unpublished Ph.D. diss., University of Georgia.

Phillips, Ulrich B., 1941. *Life and Labor in the Old South* (Boston: Little, Brown and Co.).

Rankin, Hugh F., 1965. The Colonial South. In *Writing Southern History: Essays in Historiography in Honor of Fletcher M. Green*, Arthur S. Link and Rembert W. Patrick, eds. (Baton Rouge: Louisiana State University Press).

Rouquette, Dominique, n.d. The Choctaws. Unpublished Manuscript, Louisiana State Museum Library, New Orleans.

Simkins, Francis, 1948. *The South: New and Old* (New York: Alfred A. Knopf).

——————————————————, *A History of the South,* 3rd ed. (New York: Alfred A. Knopf, 1967).

Stephenson, Wendell H., 1959. *A Basic History of the Old South* (New York: Van Nostrand Co.).

——————————————————, 1964. *Southern History in the Making: Pioneer Historians of the South* (Baton Rouge: Louisiana State University Press).

Swanton, John, 1931. *Source Material for the Social and Ceremonial Life of the Choctaw Indians,* Bureau of American Ethnology Bulletin No. 103 (Washington, D. C.: GPO).

Tindall, George Brown, ed., 1964. *The Pursuit of Southern History: Presidential Addresses of the Southern Historical Association 1935-1963* (Baton Rouge: Louisiana State University Press).

Tolbert, Charles, 1958. A Sociological Study of the Choctaw Indians in Mississippi. Unpublished Ph.D. diss., Louisiana State University.

Wharton, Vernon Lane, 1965. *The Negro in Mississippi, 1865-1890* (New York: Harper and Row).

Woodward, Grace Steele, 1963. *The Cherokees* (Norman: University of Oklahoma Press).

Comments

CHARLES CROWE

EVEN a cursory glance at the history of relations between the white man and the Indian reveals a record of unmitigated disaster for the native peoples of North America. Four centuries of white imperialism makes a depressing tale of invasion, despoilation, massacre, treachery, and random violence of all kinds. Despite the challenging work of Alden Vaughan (Columbia) and the less persuasive efforts of Bernard Sheehan (Indiana), the historical record stands generally as Helen Hunt Jackson reported it more than eighty years ago in *A Century of Dishonor*. It is not surprising that nineteenth century pretensions, accusations, and international "peace" efforts by leaders of a nation which had nearly completed the extermination of the red man reminded Otto von Bismarck of a wealthy and reformed gangster's demand for the most rigid morality from his new, respectable neighbors. More recently an Asian diplomat told an American audience that while the Western World may not have invented genocide, Americans were the only people who commemorated genocide so persistently for generations in a children's game called "cowboys and Indians." An unusually ironic contrast can be seen if one compares the bloody reality of Indian-white relations with the schoolbook tales of Pocahontas and John Smith, Squanto and the Pilgrims, and William Penn's allegedly generous policy of peace and the righteous purchase of land.

A more accurate barometer of white opinion was the maxim "the only good Indian is a dead one," held by Andrew Jackson and millions of soldiers, frontiersmen, politicians, traders, and farmers who actively took part in the dispossession of the red man. One may note partial exceptions such as Benjamin Franklin, and one may appreciate in this symposium F. N. Boney's reminder that Jefferson expressed more generous attitudes toward the original inhabitants of the continent. Even so, Franklin lacked consistency, and Jefferson's warm words

134

of praise for Indians stand in vivid contrast to his failure to stop or to slow down the continuing white war of annihilation. A related failure and a similar contrast can be found in the enormous gap between Jefferson's largely private criticisms of slavery and his active support, as planter, politician, and president, of the "peculiar institution" during an era in which it expanded from the Atlantic seaboard to the Mississippi River and beyond.

The westward expansion of slavery and the dispossession of the Indian took place almost simultaneously. After tribal removal, could the remaining red men find a place in a society of white masters and black slaves? John H. Peterson, who offers a conceptual framework for all of Indian history from the arrival of Europeans to the present, pays particular attention to Indians left behind after the great migration to Oklahoma territory. Professor Peterson argues that these Indians constituted a significant part of the history of the old South rather than being merely "cultural isolates." Certainly Peterson provides important information and insights: the loss of Choctaw literacy can be seen as a sign of general cultural shock, and the tendency of Choctaws to follow the lead of black freedmen in establishing churches and schools surely gives us an important lead. For the most part, however, we are still left with the larger realities of white devastation. Twentieth century historians in ignoring the Indian enclaves of the Southeast reflect the scorn of their forbears who drove the red men from the land. After defeat and dispossession the Indian had no place in the white man's domain or in the histories he wrote. As Ambrose Bierce suggested in *The Devil's Dictionary*, "Aborigines, n. Persons of little worth found cumbering the soil of a newly discovered country. They soon cease to cumber; they fertilize."

To consider the black man as well as the Indian is to become aware of still larger historical ironies. The enslaved African paid an extraordinarily high blood price to the imperialist who often credited the *defeated* Indian with some virtues in a comparative rhetorical context which stripped the black man of the last vestiges of humanity. For example, it is worth noting that the Spanish priest Las Casas advocated for "humanitarian" reasons the enslavement of Africans to replace the perishing Indians as forced laborers. In United States history the expansion of American democracy almost inevitably meant the advance of white racism, and the conquest and removal of Indians made it possible for whites to find admirable qualities in the defeated foe which the African lacked. Indians may have been more feared and hated on a precarious frontier during a period of active warfare, but as the frontier moved West and most Indians were pushed beyond the Mississippi hatred of the red man diminished sharply. White hatred and scorn toward blacks existed even in the absence of danger and indeed infected areas entirely or nearly devoid of black inhabitants. The fact that fewer than a hundred scattered black persons lived in Oregon during the 1850s and had never been seen by most whites did not prevent the territorial legislature from expressing a rabid Negrophobia.

Why was the hostility and the contempt more pervasive and enduring toward the black man? For one thing it was more difficult to ignore the continuing presence of the black man in the life of the nation, in patterns of work and play, songs and stereotypes, and guilt and apprehensions. The defeated and largely displaced Indian could in a sense be "forgiven," but the preservation of dominant myths of liberty, equality, and American innocence required the continuing dehumanization of the black man. Americans could not forget the long centuries of war with the Indians for the land, and though the Indian had to bear the reputation of a barbarian stripped of the land he did not merit, few Americans wished to *denigrate* (the word itself tells us much) completely an old and persistent foe for fear of making their own fighting prowess inconsequential and their final victory unworthy. White America needed to remember Indian courage and to forget black resistance. It was less disturbing to think of Tecumseh than of Nat Turner, and it was best to forget that most Africans had been wrenched from their homelands in small groups and denied the historical experience of the Indians who struggled on native soil for the existence of their land and people.

The sources of cultural strength which enabled many West Africans to survive plantation slavery while Indians commonly perished in bondage were regarded by whites not as creditable but as further evidence of cowardice and a natural aptitude for slavery. Moreover, when the existence of rebels such as Nat Turner could not be denied, their rebellions were described as "senseless violence." In other cases, the historians and the myth-makers simply "forgot" that resistance and rebellion had taken place. The Seminole Wars of the 1830s and 1840s, which might well be called "the Negro and Seminole Wars," constituted the longest, bloodiest, and most expensive Indian wars the United States ever fought. These wars raised the specter of black-red military cooperation and aroused the most intense fears among pioneer slaveholders on exposed frontiers. It is interesting to note that the Florida wars provide one of the best instances of stubborn black resistance. When peace came to Florida, some blacks made an incredible "long trek" to northern Mexico where they waged guerilla warfare for many years against Texas planters who were so skeptical about black courage that they invented fanciful stories about refugee "Marmeluke" soldiers from the remote Ottoman Empire to explain the presence of the troublesome dark-skinned fighters.

Of white imperiousness and white contacts with red and black we know much, but of initial contacts between African and Indian we know very little. Black contacts with Seminoles appear to have been mutually sympathetic ones. However, tribes such as the Cherokees and the Creeks, either initially or in imitation of the whites, behaved in a condescending manner toward blacks. In any case the most important single fact is that whites were able to establish a multi-caste system in which they were dominant over red and black. The long-range thrust of white supremacy was to compel most Indian tribes to accept grudgingly the inevitable white dominion, while trying to establish for themselves a status superior to that of the blacks. In the minds of most whites the situation was quite simple— the red man had been banished to the far West or limited to a few unimportant Eastern conclaves, and where white, red, and black happened to live in physical proximity a triple caste system existed. Yet actual social situations contained many incongruities which official ideology did not allow for. Although whites almost always granted the superiority of Indians to blacks, they frequently attempted to force Indian children into black schools. In several Mississippi counties at the turn of the century, consciousness of status and color was so intense that the ruling elite maintained four separate school systems for whites, blacks, Indians, and recent Southern Italian immigrants. If some Indians learned condescension from whites, so did some blacks: Western Indians who attended Hampton Institute and lived in "the Indian dormitory" did not escape the stigma of being considered "savages," and black soldiers who fought in Indian wars toward the end of the nineteenth century often spoke scornfully of their red enemy.

Despite all of the group hostility, a significant number of liaisons existed among whites and blacks, whites and Indians, and Indians and blacks. The offspring of these "illegitimate" unions sometimes entered social groups from which they were excluded by the official definitions of the social system. Hundreds of thousands of people with both European and African ancestors ended by "passing" as white; some persons of largely African ancestry accepted an Indian identity; and scattered individuals with largely European or Indian forebears became "black." We can learn much about color attitudes from what several scholars call "tri-ethnic" communities of men and women with varying degrees of Indian, black, and European ancestors. Faced with the reality of white domination and rejection, these people of multiple origins tried, often successfully, to maintain a separate identity as well as a social status superior to that of the blacks. It should be noted, however, that in recent years at least a few of these communities have disintegrated, that most of them exist at a level of poverty below that of the majority of blacks, that black communities have become the most dynamic sources of social change, and that leadership roles in coalitions of the poor and the non-white have been assumed largely by blacks.

Several historical discussions of the tri-ethnic communities are misleading in the use of "mestizo" and "mulatto," terms which have so much meaning in Latin-American history. Despite the scattered use of terms such as "mulatto" and "mustee" in colonial times, the two terms had little legal or formal meaning north of Mexico in the nineteenth century. According to most American laws and all official creeds, men were implacably and unchangingly white, black, or red. By contrast, in the complex social hierarchies of most Latin national societies of the New World, many status levels existed, and the status of a particular individual was determined by wealth, education, ancestry, and political power as well as by color. Thus, unlike the United States, Brazil and Cuba allowed wealthy and powerful dark-skinned men to rise to very high positions.

The existence of American "tri-ethnic" communities sprang from the iron determination of whites to continue the debasement of blacks, as well as from the desperate striving of "mixed" communities to avoid at all costs the despised label of "Negro." The study of these communities tells us important things but we must remember that they were scattered and isolated enclaves, often unknown a few miles away from their location and lacking significant influence on the history of American society. Presumably an iron wall of total separation existed between white and black, and whites almost invariably tried to deny the obvious evidence of their senses by acting as if Americans came in only one of the two totally opposite and different colors. The inevitable confusion appeared, among other places and times, during the suppression of the Philippine insurrection when white soldiers commonly spoke of Philippinos as "niggers." Yet the same soldiers back in America would almost certainly have made a rigid distinction between "Indian" and "Negro." When lawyers tried to work with the problem, they sometimes said that a Negro was a person with one-quarter, one-eighth, one-sixteenth, one-thirty-second, or "any known trace" of African ancestry. White public opinion also granted the all-conquering nature of "Negro blood," often to the extent of asserting that "one drop" would overwhelm gallons of "European blood." Every village and county which contained both peoples had its secrets of black-white kinships, but whites continued to stress the terrible black "biological threat" to the white race. Presumably "race-mixing" and "mongrelization of the races," a fate worse than death, had never happened and should be prevented at any cost.

Yet the actual conduct of whites frequently conflicted with their own passionately expounded rhetoric. For example, the fact of race mixture was often acknowledged to demonstrate that any merit or ability displayed by a black person could be attributed to white ancestry. Before the Civil War many planters emancipated those slaves closest to their own color, and a much more common means of expressing color preference was to allow light-skinned slaves to escape the brutal conditions of field labor by becoming house servants. After Civil War and Reconstruction, access to better occupations such as barbering, farming, catering, and the skilled trades was given much more freely to black persons of "mixed" ancestry. Moreover, these economic patterns were reinforced in countless ways by a culture which made "black" synonymous with sin, death, dishonesty, treachery, and ugliness and associated "white" with God, heaven, angels, virtue, purity, morality, and beauty. Nevertheless the prosperous black who traded on a lighter skin color to the extent of forgetting his membership in a subordinate caste courted death. Favors promised by the white man to the more industrious and the "less offensive" often turned out to be the promises of, as the expression goes, Indian givers. Americans insisted both on keeping blacks in the one rank assigned to all persons with known African ancestors, and at the same time they acted in complete contradiction to this principle by making a number of color distinctions in daily life.

The common devotion of every social class in the dominant caste to capitalism and white supremacy becomes evident in Professor Boney's paper. Joseph L. Brent tends to support Boney's case as well as to give information about the insistent demands for both equality and higher status which helped to make white racism functional. Perhaps it will be best to clarify the point by making more explicit the nature of the clash between official ideology and conflicting social experiences. White Americans could have their cake and eat it too by preaching universal equality while simultaneously reaping status gains from the maintenance of servile castes.

The American creed of "equality of opportunity" often seemed a mere euphemism for the frantic scramble for wealth, status, and power in which a few would gain a great deal of "equality," or to speak more plainly, ascendancy over others. These basic contradictions have made realistic assessments of American society hard to come by. Americans, seeing themselves as an innocent people, found it difficult to acknowledge the fact that the continent was gained by the near extermination of the Indian, the exploitation of poor whites and immigrants, and the oppression of black people. Because America is by definition the land of freedom and equality, the elaborate system of status and caste as well as the long history of imperialism and racial oppression must be denied. Recently, however, the emergence of oppressed minorities, particularly blacks, has thrust the nation toward a confrontation with its own history which must end in a restructuring of American society or in massive civil strife.

In the final analysis American history is a part of Western history, and racism must be traced to its European roots. The United States did develop a much more fanatical domestic version of white supremacy, but American racism can best be seen in the context of world history. For generations "civilized" Europeans expressed irritation over white American arrogance toward the black middle class: in 1850 Frederick Douglass could hope to gain the sympathetic ear of English aristocrats over indignities he suffered after his flight from slavery; in 1918 French army officers could express disgust over the determination of white Americans to treat black officers as subhuman; Richard Wright could realistically hope to find a life largely free of harrassment by fleeing to Paris in 1945; and even today black Mississippians can evoke concerned responses among millions of Europeans. Protestations of European "innocence," however, bear a strong resemblance to similar myths about innocent Americans. In the early years of the twentieth century it would have been easy to raise money for American lynch victims in Brussels but very difficult to get a hearing over the massacre of hundreds of thousands of people in the Belgian Congo. For centuries white European imperialists sacked the world and grew fat with arrogance at the expense of "the lesser breeds without." For many generations France, England, and other Western nations enjoyed a growing domestic equality and liberty, while the very same nations continued the colonial oppression of the Afro-Asian and Latin American peoples of the world. Today, thoughtful men know that the future must be different and that the system of Western exploitation of the world must be dismantled completely to make possible a humane existence for red, white, black, and yellow.

The Contributors

F. N. Boney is associate professor of history at the University of Georgia. He has published two books and 20 articles on various aspects of Southern history, and now he is investigating slavery in Virginia and Georgia in the late ante-bellum period.

Joseph L. Brent III is associate professor in the Department of History at Federal City College. His principal field of study is the history of ideas in the United States, and his main interest lies in the philosophy and methods of history. He has done work on Charles Pierce, the mind of the South, and Afro-American issues, among other topics. He has published on the South and is co-editor of *The Process of American History*.

Charles Crowe is associate professor of history at the University of Georgia and a member of the editorial board of *The Journal of Negro History*. The author of three books, he has done research on New England trancendentalism, American socialism, and more recently on black-white racial violence.

Louis De Vorsey, Jr. is acting head of the Department of Geography at the University of Georgia. His major research interests include the historical geography and historical cartography of the Southeast during the eighteenth and early nineteenth centuries.

Charles H. Fairbanks is chairman of the Department of Anthropology at the University of Florida. His primary interests are Southeastern archaeology, including colonial archaeology, cultural evolution, and revitalization movements in the Southeastern United States.

Mary R. Haas is professor of linguistics and program coordinator of the Survey of California and Other Indian Languages at the University of California, Berkeley. She has done field work on several Southeastern languages, particularly Tunica, Natchez, Creek, and Koasati, and also on the languages of Southeast Asia, especially Thai and Burmese. Her publications include articles on comparative (genetic) and areal linguistics and on linguistic classificatory systems (e.g. noun classifiers and classificatory verbs). A recent book is *The Prehistory of Languages.*

David J. Hally is assistant professor of anthropology in the Department of Sociology and Anthropology at the University of Georgia. His topical interests include archaeological field methods and settlement archaeology. His area interest is the Southeastern United States.

Charles Hudson is associate professor of anthropology in the Department of Sociology and Anthropology at the University of Georgia. His main interests are in the Indians of the Southeastern United States and in folk belief systems.

John H. Peterson, Jr. is assistant professor in the Department of Sociology and Anthropology and assistant anthropologist in the Social Science Research Center at Mississippi State University. His theoretical interest in pluralism is reflected in his research in ethnohistory, contemporary community, minority relations, and applied anthropology in education and natural resource development. In addition to applied research, he has done field work among the Choctaw and among Negro and white Southerners.

William S. Pollitzer is associate professor of anatomy at the University of North Carolina at Chapel Hill. He also serves the Department of Anthropology, the Genetics Training Program, and the Carolina Population Center. His main research interests are in the application of genetic factors to the problems of physical anthropology. His field studies have included isolated populations of Negroes, Indians, and persons of mixed ancestry in the Southeastern United States.

William S. Willis, Jr. is an associate professor in the Department of Anthropology at Southern Methodist University and a research associate with the Smithsonian Institution. He is also a visiting associate professor in the Graduate Department of Anthropology at Columbia University. His main interests are in Black-Indian-White relations in Southeastern North America and in problems in the development of anthropology.

Southern Anthropological
Society Proceedings

Thomas Weaver (ed.), *Essays on Medical Anthropology*, 1968, No. 1. $3.00

Elizabeth M. Eddy (ed.), *Urban Anthropology: Research Perspectives and Strategies*, 1968, No. 2. $3.00

Stephen A. Tyler (ed.), *Concepts and Assumptions in Contemporary Anthropology*, 1969, No. 3. $3.00

J. Kenneth Morland (ed.), *The Not So Solid South: Anthropological Studies in a Regional Subculture*, 1971, No. 4. $3.75

Charles Hudson (ed.), *Red, White, and Black: Symposium on Indians in the Old South*, 1971, No. 5. $3.75